English

Name _____

Write each set of words in the correct order to make a sentence. The first word is underlined.

1. floors our in <u>There</u> school are two

_____

2. is mascot a school bulldog <u>Our</u>

_____

3. kindergarten just sister started <u>My</u>

_____

4. <u>Math</u> is subject favorite my

_____

5. on street <u>What</u> is school your

_____

6. minivan drives blue <u>My</u> a teacher

_____

7. delicious cafeteria <u>Our</u> pizza serves

_____

8. your name is principal's <u>What</u>

_____

9. in <u>We</u> hockey gym played floor

_____

10. May in show <u>Our</u> art school had an

_____

11. won spelling friend <u>My</u> contest best the

_____

12. <u>I</u> perfect award received an attendance for

_____

Chance

English

Name _____

Number each set of words in alphabetical order.

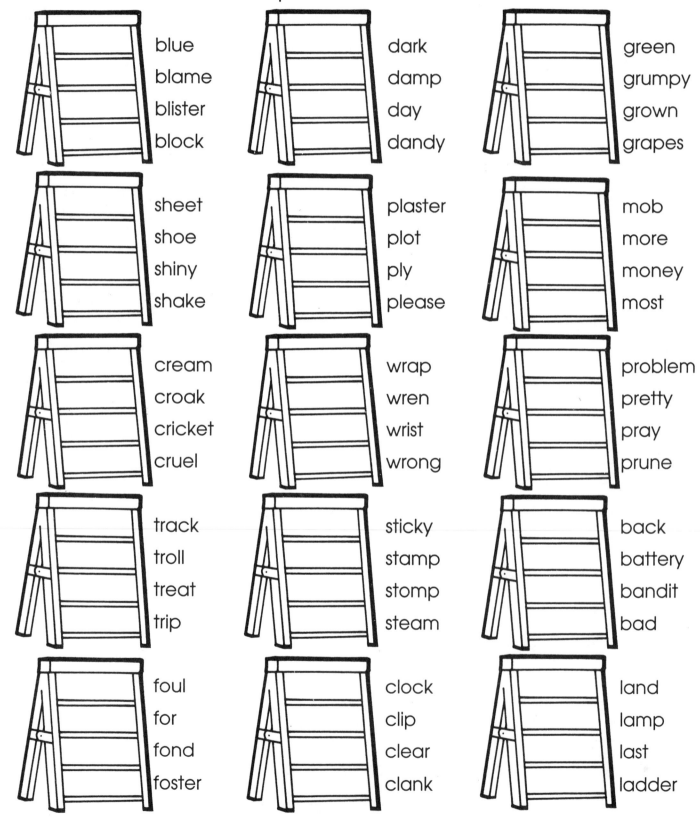

blue
blame
blister
block

dark
damp
day
dandy

green
grumpy
grown
grapes

sheet
shoe
shiny
shake

plaster
plot
ply
please

mob
more
money
most

cream
croak
cricket
cruel

wrap
wren
wrist
wrong

problem
pretty
pray
prune

track
troll
treat
trip

sticky
stamp
stomp
steam

back
battery
bandit
bad

foul
for
fond
foster

clock
clip
clear
clank

land
lamp
last
ladder

English

Name _____

Add the correct punctuation mark in the color shown on the crayon.

orange

green

red

blue

1. What are the colors of the U.S.A. flag

2. Scarlet is a shade of red

3. I was tickled pink at the surprise party

4. Cut out the orange triangles

5. Do not cross the red line

6. Tim won a brand new black dirt bike

7. Who wore the purple and blue coat

8. Red, yellow, and blue are primary colors

9. Turquoise is a bluish-green color

10. Put the pink bow on the present

11. An emerald is a green gem

12. What color is made by combining red with blue

13. I was so mad that I saw red

14. Mix the white and red to make pink

15. A prism gives off many beautiful colors

16. Is cinnamon a shade of brown

17. Water is usually blue on maps and globes

English

Name _____

Draw a pair of scissors between the subject and predicate of each sentence.

1. The oldest existing pair of scissors is from Egypt.

2. Scissors were made around 300 B.C.

3. Scissors are two knife blades joined together.

4. They are an example of a lever.

5. Barbers use scissors to cut hair.

6. Early scissors were one piece of metal with two blades connected by a curved handle.

7. Shears are scissors with blades six inches long or longer.

8. Pinking shears cut in a zigzag pattern.

9. Left-handed people can buy left-handed scissors.

10. Today, some scissors can even cut a scalloped edge.

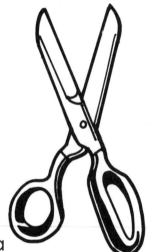

Add a subject or predicate to each group of words to make a complete sentence.

the soccer team	chased the ball
won the big game	the black and white ball

1. _____

2. _____

3. _____

4. _____

English

Name _____

chance

In the lower bunk bed, write a synonym for the word in the upper bunk bed. Then color the bed containing the word that would come first in ABC order.

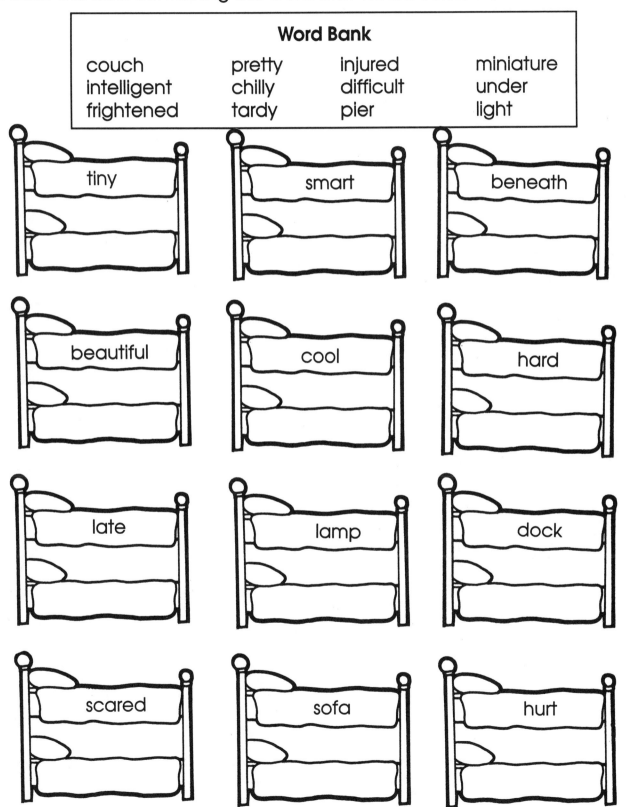

Word Bank

couch	pretty	injured	miniature
intelligent	chilly	difficult	under
frightened	tardy	pier	light

tiny

smart

beneath

beautiful

cool

hard

late

lamp

dock

scared

sofa

hurt

English

Name _____

Find the matching antonym for each word listed under the anthills. Then draw the correct number of ants on each anthill to show the number of the matching antonym.

1. under	5. hot	9. lower	13. thin
2. south	6. awake	10. hard	14. rested
3. play	7. dirty	11. leave	15. last
4. empty	8. dull	12. melt	16. light

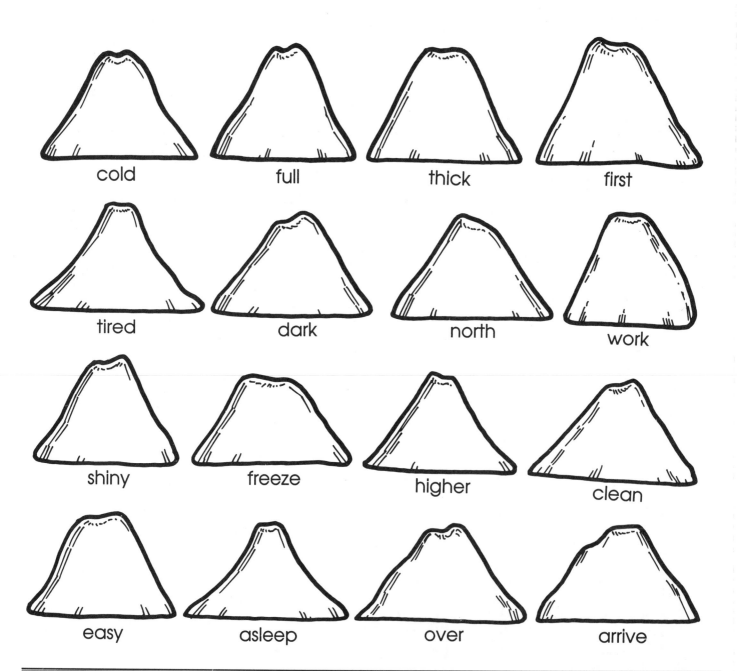

cold full thick first

tired dark north work

shiny freeze higher clean

easy asleep over arrive

English

Name _____

Circle the correct homonyms for Hairy Harry.

1. Harry (new, knew) all about homonyms.

2. (Its, It's) too late to get your hair cut today.

3. Can you (buy, by) me a new brush, Mom?

4. (They're, Their, There) is no more shampoo.

5. Can a sheep dog (sea, see) through all of his hair?

6. Harry's hair (blew, blue) wildly in the wind.

7. Barbers often (ewes, use) clippers.

8. (Here, Hear) is your blow dryer, Harry.

9. (Eye, I) can tell you have a new hairstyle.

10. No one (knows, nose) why Harry spiked his hair.

11. Hairy Harry once (died, dyed) his hair green!

12. (Wheel, We'll) never see Hairy Harry bald.

13. A (bare, bear) head does not appeal to Harry.

14. Harry had a (tail, tale) as part of his hairstyle.

15. His hair got so thin you could see (threw, through) to his scalp.

16. Harry's shortest haircut was before he had (to, too, two) swim in a meet.

17. It (seams, seems) that Harry lost the swim meet.

18. Have you ever (heard, herd) of anyone as crazy as Hairy Harry?

19. Did you (chews, choose) your hairstyle?

English

Name _____

Read the dictionary entry for *dugout,* then follow the directions below.

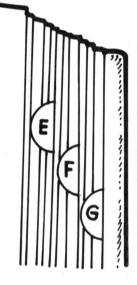

dryly   **duty**

dug•out (dŭg´out)*N.* ¹ A rough shelter or dwelling formed by digging into the side of a hill or trench. *During war, soldiers use dugouts for protection against bullets and bombs.* ² A small shelter at either side of a baseball field, used by players not on the field. ³ Boat made by hollowing out a large log.

1. How many definitions are given for dugout? _____

2. Circle in orange the part of speech dugout is.

3. Underline in blue the example sentence for the first meaning.

4. How many syllables are in dugout? _____

5. What are the guidewords? _____ _____

6. Which syllable is accented? _____

7. Give the number of the definition of *dugout* as used in each of the following sentences.

   a. The Indians used dugout canoes. _____

   b. The soldiers hid in the dugout. _____

   c. A dugout was carved from a large log. _____

   d. There were 25 players in the dugout. _____

   e. The dugout was their shelter from bullets. _____

   f. The baseball players stayed in the dugout during the rain delay. _____

English

Name _____

Underline each noun. Then, in the boxes, draw the symbol for each noun in the order it appears in the sentence.

 = person   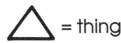 = place   = thing

1. Two boys raced their skateboards down the street.

2. My grandpa lives in Chicago.

3. Dad bought a new minivan in Michigan.

4. The football sailed over the goalpost.

5. The sled glided down the hill.

6. We have a telephone in the kitchen and in the den.

7. Our cat and dog sleep in the garage.

8. My sister returned her book to the library.

9. Pizza and pop are my favorite treats.

10. Our teacher and principal ate in the cafeteria.

11. Michael owned two basketballs.

12. Mom bought my glasses at the mall.

13. The coach awarded medals to the players.

English

Name _____

Draw a red  around each singular noun, and a yellow around each plural noun. Then add green plants and blue waves to the fish tank.

starfish

tadpole

eggs

seaweed

seas

whale

lakes

snail

turtles

bubbles

guppies

tanks

minnow

sea horse

lilypad

seashells

dolphins

IF8785 Third Grade in Review

English

Name _____

Match each common and proper noun. Then, before each common noun, write your own proper noun.

Example:

__**B. Clinton**__   1. president

_____   2. restaurant

_____   3. soda pop

_____   4. athletic shoe

_____   5. religion

_____   6. state

_____   7. dog

_____   8. store

_____   9. airline

_____   10. continent

_____   11. author

_____   12. baseball team

_____   13. bird

_____   14. soap

_____   15. cartoon character

_____   16. city

_____   17. car

_____   18. college

____ Beverly Cleary

____ Delta

____ Canada goose

____ Los Angeles

_1._ Abraham Lincoln

____ Nike

____ Ivory

____ German shepherd

____ Catholic

____ Florida

____ Ohio State University

____ Pepsi

____ Europe

____ J.C. Penney

____ Snoopy

____ Toronto Blue Jays

____ Toyota

____ Taco Bell

English

Name _____

In each 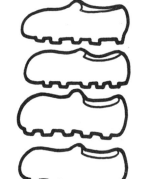 write a pronoun that could take the place of the underlined noun(s).

Example: (He) <u>Bob</u> saw the movie twice.

1. The cat chased <u>the cat's</u> tail.

2. <u>Grandma and Grandpa</u> moved to Florida.

3. <u>My sister</u> was born in July.

4. We gave the puppy to <u>our neighbors</u>.

5. <u>Rick and I</u> played soccer on Monday.

6. <u>Ashley's</u> mom will drive us to school.

7. Please give your coat to <u>Kim and me</u>.

8. <u>The chair</u> was missing one rung.

9. We played against <u>Justin's</u> team.

10. <u>My family and I</u> went to Disney World.

11. Take your homework to <u>Mr. Strayer</u>.

12. <u>My cousins</u> live in California.

13. We went to see <u>Sue</u> in the hospital.

14. Brent gave his lunch to <u>Greg and me</u>.

15. <u>Megan and Barb</u> played tennis.

16. Where was <u>the car</u> supposed to be parked?

English

Name _____

Write the abbreviation above each word.

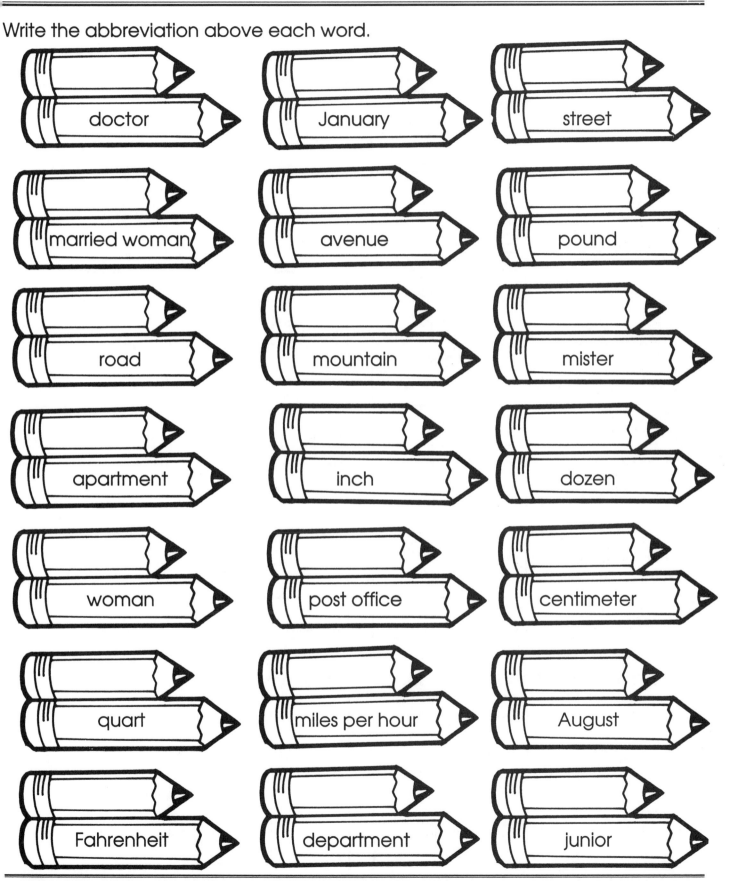

doctor

January

street

married woman

avenue

pound

road

mountain

mister

apartment

inch

dozen

woman

post office

centimeter

quart

miles per hour

August

Fahrenheit

department

junior

English

Name _____

Write two verbs for each object.

Example:

fly
land

_____
_____

_____
_____

_____
_____

_____
_____

_____
_____

_____
_____

_____
_____

_____
_____

_____
_____

_____
_____

_____
_____

Now draw something that goes with each pair of verbs.

hiss slither	gallop trot	fly chirp	slam lock

English

Name _____

Write a letter to the President of the United States. Then draw a colored box around each part of a friendly letter as directed below.

_____

_____

_____

Dear President _____ ,

_____

_____

_____

_____

_____

_____

_____

_____

_____

_____

_____ ,

_____

signature—green   **closing**—yellow
greeting—blue   **heading**—orange
body—red

English

Name _____

Write two adjectives in each pair of glasses to describe each noun.

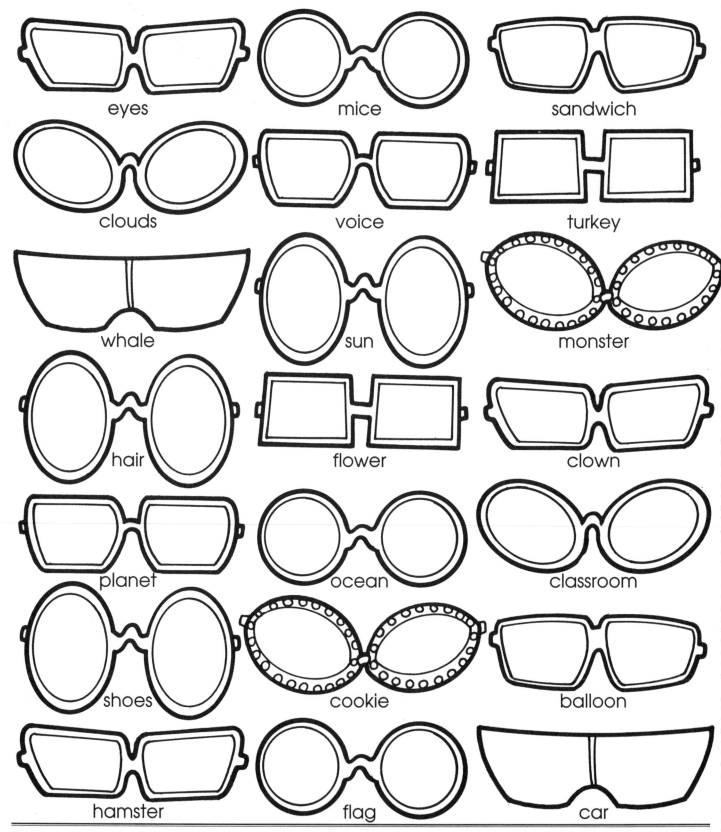

eyes

mice

sandwich

clouds

voice

turkey

whale

sun

monster

hair

flower

clown

planet

ocean

classroom

shoes

cookie

balloon

hamster

flag

car

16

IF8785 Third Grade in Review

English

Name _____

Write each adverb in the correct clue box.

Where?

_____
_____
_____
_____
_____
_____
_____
_____

How?

_____
_____
_____
_____
_____
_____
_____
_____

When?

_____
_____
_____
_____
_____
_____
_____
_____

Adverb File

outside	somewhere	tomorrow	anywhere	nervously
slowly	loudly	there	proudly	here
yesterday	soon	inside	then	calmly
now	up	quietly	late	early
quickly	sneakily	once	down	under

17

Reading

Name _____

Use the number equations to help you write compound words. The first word is in Group A, the second is in Group B. Write the compound word under each ice cream cone.

Group A		Group B	
1. grand	7. tea	1. butter	7. fish
2. cross	8. peanut	2. boat	8. word
3. cat	9. river	3. ground	9. flake
4. flower	10. basket	4. bed	10. mother
5. snow	11. water	5. kettle	11. ball
6. corn	12. play	6. cob	12. pot

IF8785 Third Grade in Review

Reading

Name _____

Get on the right track with contractions. Write the contraction for each pair of words in the matching car of the train.

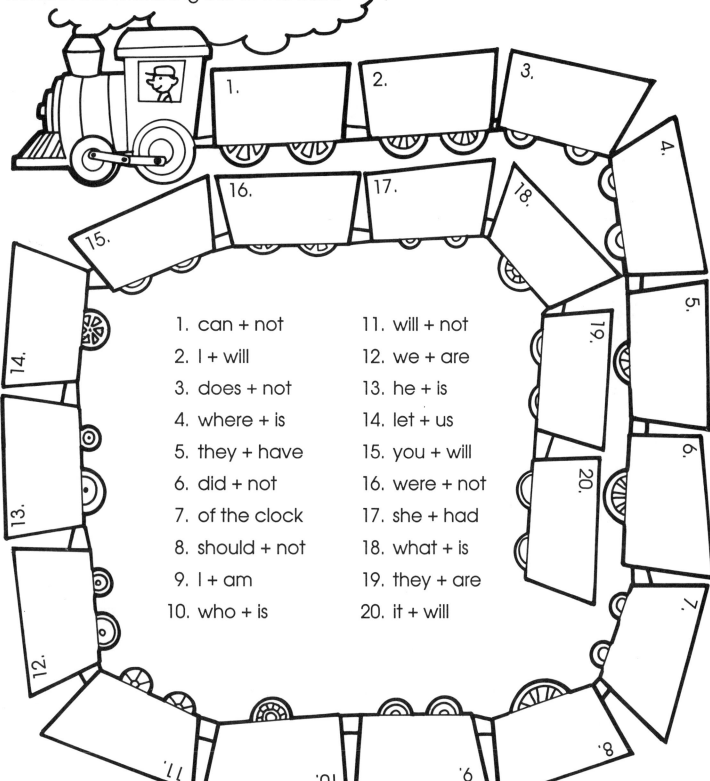

1. can + not
2. I + will
3. does + not
4. where + is
5. they + have
6. did + not
7. of the clock
8. should + not
9. I + am
10. who + is

11. will + not
12. we + are
13. he + is
14. let + us
15. you + will
16. were + not
17. she + had
18. what + is
19. they + are
20. it + will

IF8785 Third Grade in Review

Reading

Name _____

Write a prefix for each base word. Then write the points scored by using that prefix. Tally your final score on the scoreboard.

2   4   5   1   3

pre   dis   im   un   re   Final Score

_____ connect   _____ view   _____ cover   _____ fix
_____ points   _____ points   _____ points   _____ points

_____ polite   _____ caring   _____ call   _____ finished
_____ points   _____ points   _____ points   _____ points

_____ make   _____ tend   _____ believable   _____ bound
_____ points   _____ points   _____ points   _____ points

_____ start   _____ heat   _____ charge   _____ kind
_____ points   _____ points   _____ points   _____ points

_____ possible   _____ tied   _____ locked   _____ port
_____ points   _____ points   _____ points   _____ points

Reading

Name _____

Write a suffix for each base word. Color the snakes as shown.

ing
(red/blue)

ly
(yellow/green)

ful
(orange/brown)

less
(purple/pink)

er
(black/white)

slow _____   care _____   cup _____   jump _____

home _____   soft _____   quick _____   lift _____

weight _____   thank _____   hand _____   color _____

tank _____   play _____   teach _____   sick _____

sleep _____   light _____   watch _____   help _____

Reading

Name _____

Count the syllables in each word. Draw that number of gumballs in each machine.

gumballs

rapidly

important

unsuccessful

video

picnic

fantastic

machine

disappearing

bubble

camera

treat

beautiful

motorcycle

lightning

gasoline

encyclopedia

syllable

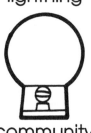
community

camper

pillow

dictionary

orange

title

Reading

Name _____

Number each group of sentences in the correct order. Then illustrate the action/event that matches the number shown in each box.

1

_____ Then he cut them out.

_____ Finally, he hung them in the gallery.

_____ He glued the sketches onto a thick red border.

_____ The artist drew two sketches of flowers.

4

_____ She glued the tiles to an oak board.

_____ An artist collected small colored tiles to make a mosaic.

_____ They formed a beautiful pattern!

_____ She sorted the tiles into color groups.

2

_____ Finally, he added a beautiful sunset behind the mountains.

_____ Then he painted color into the mountains.

_____ The artist picked up his pallet and stood before his easel.

_____ He sketched where the mountains would be.

3

_____ The sculptor removed the wet clay from the plastic bag.

_____ He glazed, then baked the vase in the kiln.

_____ He formed the clay into a vase on the potter's wheel.

_____ He rolled the wet red clay into a large ball.

Reading

Name _____

Write the long vowel for each word. Draw the object inside each pyramid.

Example:

__a__ ngel

h ___ se

___ ce cream

b ___ ne

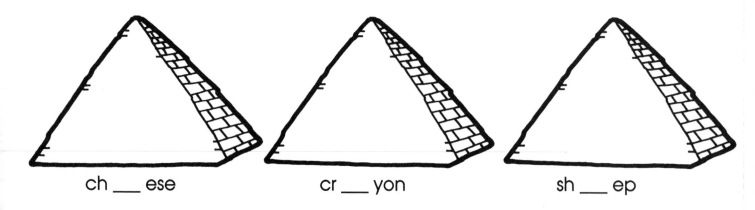

ch ___ ese

cr ___ yon

sh ___ ep

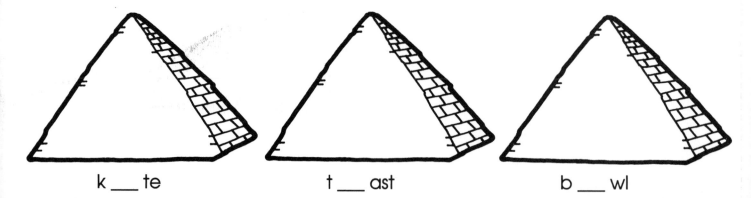

k ___ te

t ___ ast

b ___ wl

Reading

Name _____

  ă    ĕ    ĭ    ŏ   ŭ

Write the missing vowel for each word. Then draw the correct short vowel pattern on each teepee.

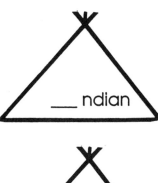 __ndian

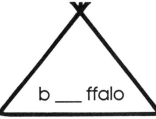 b __ ffalo

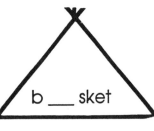 b __ sket

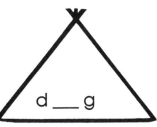 d __ g

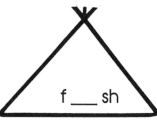 f ___ sh

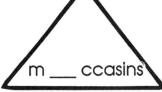 m ___ ccasins

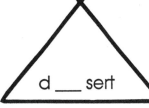 d ___ sert

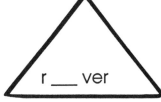 r __ ver

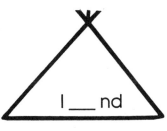 l __ nd

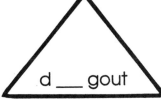 d __ gout

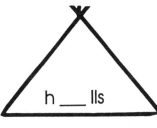 h __ lls

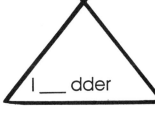 l __ dder

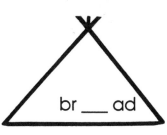 br __ ad

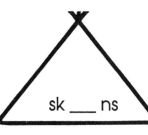 sk __ ns

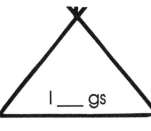 l __ gs

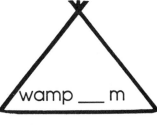 wamp __ m

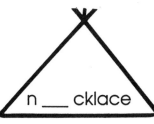 n __ cklace

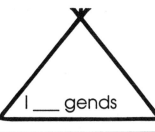 l __ gends

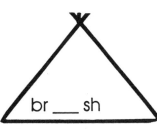 br ___ sh

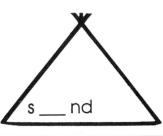 s __ nd

IF8785 Third Grade in Review

Reading

Name _____

 oa    **ou**    **ai**    **ea**    **ie**

Write the missing vowel pair on each line. Draw the correct hat on each face.

st __ __ m   r __ __ nd   t __ __ d

afr __ __ d   p __ __ crust   w __ __ st

rel __ __ f   gr __ __ nd hog   ch __ __ f

ah __ __ d   t __ __ ster   qu __ __ l

Reading

Name _____

Add the correct **r-controlled vowel**. Then write the words in the correct house.

c ___ ___ penter   c ___ ___ pet   refrigerat ___ ___

b ___ ___ thplace   r ___ ___ al   b ___ ___ dbath

f ___ ___ niture   s ___ ___ vey   wallpap ___ ___

st ___ ___ m   st ___ ___ eroom   f ___ ___ eplace

flow ___ ___ s   libr ___ ___ y   carp___ ___t

g ___ ___ age   c ___ ___ tains   dishwash ___ ___

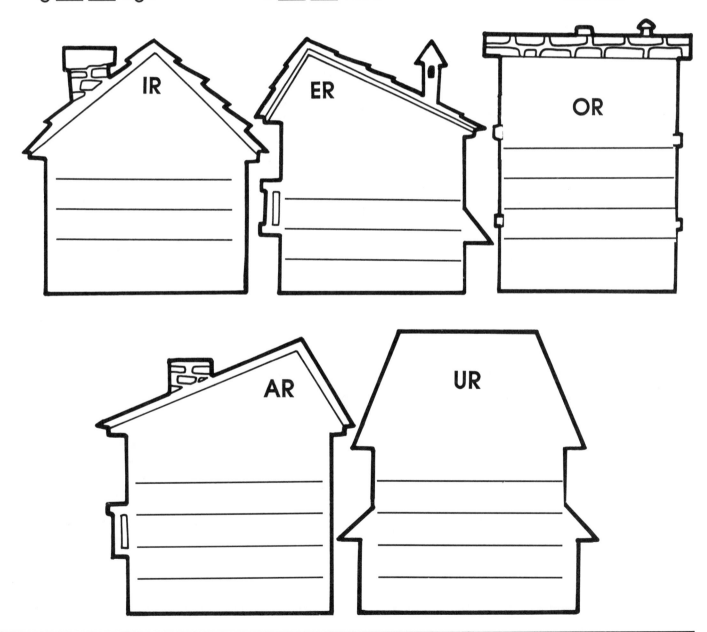

Houses labeled: IR, ER, OR, AR, UR

Reading

Name _____

Write the missing blend in each word. Then color the bow the correct color.

bl (red)	**tr** (green)	**pr** (blue)	**st** (yellow)	**fl** (orange)	**cl** (pink)	**dr** (purple)

 ___ esent

 ___ ess

 ___ owers

 ___ ock

 ___ amps

 ___ easure

 ___ ums

 ___ ouse

 ___ izes

 ___ ippers

 ___ othes

 ___ own

 ___ opwatch

 ___ ender

 ___ actor

 ___ incess

 ___ ashlight

 ___ ickers

 ___ anket

 ___ ove

Reading

Name _____

Write the missing consonant blend.

ph	ck	sh	rt	ct
st	nt	nd	ld	ch

Example:

(a plate)
di ___ ___

(noise)
sou ___ ___

(hairless)
ba ___ ___

(1, 2, 3 . . .)
cou ___ ___

(tilt)
sla ___ ___

(a chart)
gra ___ ___

(begin)
sta ___ ___

(save)
colle ___ ___

(signature)
autogra ___ ___

(vegetable)
squa ___ ___

(sofa)
cou ___ ___

(breakfast bread)
toa ___ ___

(fast)
qui ___ ___

(direction)
we ___ ___

(join)
conne ___ ___

Reading

Name _____

Read the **effect** (what happened) for each fairy tale below and write its **cause** (why something happened).

1. Jack and Jill went up the hill ...

   cause: _____

2. Old Mother Hubbard went to her cupboard ...

   cause: _____

3. Goldilocks ran from the Three Bears' house ...

   cause: _____

4. The Ugly Duckling felt very sad ...

   cause: _____

5. The Troll wanted to eat the three Billy Goats ...

   cause: _____

6. The Tortoise won the race ...

   cause: _____

7. Sleeping Beauty finally awakened ...

   cause: _____

8. The Big Bad Wolf huffed and puffed ...

   cause: _____

9. Little Red Riding Hood walked through the woods ...

   cause: _____

10. Cinderella went to the ball ...

    cause: _____

Reading

Name _____

If the statement about a president is a **fact** that can be proven, write a red **F** before the number. If it is an **opinion**, what someone believes or thinks to be true, write a blue **O** before the number.

_____ 1. John Adams was the first president to live in the White House.

_____ 2. Our nation's capital was named after George Washington.

_____ 3. Abe Lincoln was the smartest president.

_____ 4. William H. Harrison was president the shortest time.

_____ 5. John F. Kennedy was the most popular president.

_____ 6. James Monroe was the fifth president.

_____ 7. No one was fairer than Dwight D. Eisenhower.

_____ 8. Ulysses S. Grant's real initials were H.U.G.

_____ 9. Franklin D. Roosevelt made the best laws for our country.

_____ 10. Teddy bears were named after Theodore Roosevelt.

_____ 11. Grover Cleveland had the nicest daughter.

_____ 12. Richard Nixon was the first president to resign.

_____ 13. Andrew Jackson liked train travel the best.

_____ 14. John Tyler had 15 children.

_____ 15. No president did a better job than Thomas Jefferson.

_____ 16. Bill Clinton was the most musical president.

Reading

Name _____

Write the missing double consonants.

le  er   a  ount   ru  er

gi  le   ca  ing   bu  le

hi  ing   wa  le   ha  er

no  le   go  le   babysi  er

wi  le   sto  ing   pu  le

gue  ing   ki  en   ra  oon

hi 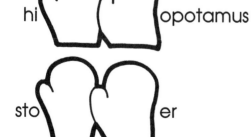 opotamus   a  le   o  er

sto 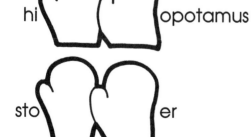 er   spa  ow   ga  on

Reading

Name _____

1. Draw a red and yellow beach umbrella in the SW corner.

2. Under the umbrella draw two polka-dotted beach towels.

3. Draw a blue and green sailboat in the center of the ocean.

4. To the left of the sailboat draw three fish.

5. Draw a refreshment stand in the SE corner of the beach.

6. Draw six seashells along the coastline.

7. Draw a purple and pink surfboard tied to the sailboat.

8. Make a sandcastle in the center of the beach area.

9. Draw two children, one on each side of the sandcastle.

10. Color several blue and green wave lines (〰) in the water.

11. Make up a name for the beach. Draw a sign with the beach's name left of the refreshment stand.

Creative Writing

Name _____

Think of ten funny, creative reasons
kids might give their teacher for not
doing their homework.

I couldn't do my homework because ...

1. _____
2. _____
3. _____
4. _____
5. _____
6. _____
7. _____
8. _____
9. _____
10. _____

Write a short story telling about a time you didn't complete your homework.
Give the reason why and explain what happened because it wasn't completed.

_____

_____

_____

_____

_____

_____

_____

_____

Creative Writing

Name _____

Become a composer. Write your own silly songs using these familiar melodies.

I. **(Yankee Doodle)**

_____ _____ came to _____

Upon a _____ _____ ,

He stuck a _____ in his _____

And called it _____ .

_____ _____ keep it up, _____

_____ _____

Mind the music and the _____

And with the _____ be _____ .

II. **(Three Blind Mice)**

Three _____ _____ , Three _____ _____ ,

See how they _____ , See how they _____ ,

They all ran after the _____ 's _____ ,

Who cut off their tails with a _____ _____ ,

Did you ever see such a _____ in your life,

As three _____ _____ .

III. **(If You're Happy and You Know It)**

If you're happy and you know it, _____ _____ _____

If you're happy and you know it, _____ _____ _____

If you're happy and you know it,

Then your _____ will surely _____ _____ ,

If you're happy and you know it, _____ _____ _____ .

Creative Writing

Name _____

This letter fell into the wrong paws! Snoopy tore and ate part of Charlie Brown's letter to Lucy. Finish the letter for Charlie.

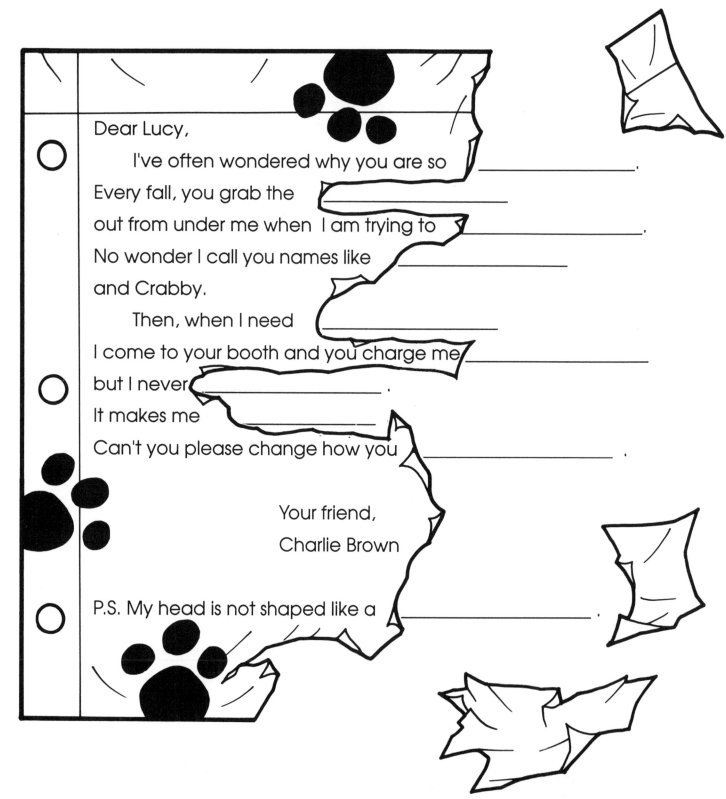

Dear Lucy,

    I've often wondered why you are so _____.

Every fall, you grab the _____

out from under me when I am trying to _____.

No wonder I call you names like _____

and Crabby.

    Then, when I need _____

I come to your booth and you charge me _____

but I never _____.

It makes me _____

Can't you please change how you _____ .

        Your friend,

        Charlie Brown

P.S. My head is not shaped like a _____.

Creative Writing

Name _____

Create your own cartoons for these comic strips. Use speech bubbles.

Create a cartoon starring your own pet.

Creative Writing

Name _____

For your birthday this year, you were allowed to take three friends on a hot-air balloon adventure for one day. Write about who you took and where you went. Use details to answer who, what, when, where, and why.

HAPPY BIRTHDAY TO YOU!

_____

_____

_____

_____

_____

_____

_____

_____

_____

Creative Writing

Name _____

If you could plan one day's meals consisting of all junk food, what would you eat? Write and illustrate your menu.

Breakfast

_____
_____
_____
_____
_____

Lunch

_____
_____
_____
_____
_____

Dinner

_____
_____
_____
_____
_____

Critical Thinking

Name _____

Let's see how much you know. Answer each question very carefully.

1. Who does the Washington Monument honor? _____

2. How many cookies are in an empty cookie jar? _____

3. How many minutes are in a 3-minute hourglass? _____

4. A pair of shoes is how many shoes? _____

5. Where was the Vietnam War fought? _____

6. The Ohio River was named for which state? _____

7. How do you spell hippopotamus? _____

8. What was President John F. Kennedy's last name? _____

9. All aboard Flight 746 died in the crash. How many survivors were there?
   _____

10. What is the product of 9 x 8 x 7 x 6 x 5 x 4 x 3 x 2 x 1 x 0? _____

11. Lay a penny, nickel, and dime on the table to help you work this problem. Jordan's mom had three kids. She named the first one Penny, the second one Nickel. What did she name the third child? _____

12. How many pigs were in the tale, *The Three Little Pigs*? _____

13. Who wrote the autobiography of Abraham Lincoln? _____

14. How many months have 28 days? _____

Math

Name _____

Choose a partner. Each of you will need a copy of the grid. You can share a pair of dice. One player rolls the dice. Add the numbers and enter the answer in the correct square on the grid. If that square is full, you lose your turn. The first player to fill the grid wins.

Example: + 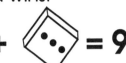 = 9   (Enter in either the square for 3 + 6 or 6 + 3)

+	6	2	5	4	1	3
5						
1						
3	9					
6						
2						
4						

         IF8785 Third Grade in Review

Math

Name _____

Use the code on the satellite panels to answer the problems.

Example: ⌐ – X = _12 – 6 = 6_

4 =)	9 = U	14 = L
5 = ⊂	10 = (	15 = △
6 = X	11 = ⊏	16 = □
7 = ⌐	12 = ⌐	17 = ⊃
8 = O	13 = ▽	18 = ⊓

1. O –) = _____
2. ▽ – ⊂ = _____
3. ⊏ – ⌐ = _____
4. □ – U = _____
5. (– ⊂ = _____
6. ⌐ –) = _____
7. ⊃ – U = _____
8. ⌐ – ⊂ = _____
9. (– X = _____
10. L – O = _____
11. ▽ –) = _____
12. △ – X = _____
13. □ – O = _____
14. ⊓ – U = _____

15. △ – ⌐ = _____
16. L – ⌐ = _____
17. ⌐ – X = _____
18. (– ⊂ = _____
19. L – U = _____
20. ⊏ – ⊂ = _____
21. ▽ – ⌐ = _____
22. □ – ⌐ = _____
23. ⌐ – O = _____
24. ⊃ – O = _____
25. △ – U = _____
26. ▽ – O = _____
27. L – X = _____
28. ⌐ – ⌐ = _____

Math

Name _____

Work each problem.

6	7	5	9	3	8	7
9	4	7	6	8	4	5
+ 5	+ 8	+ 4	+ 7	+ 5	+ 8	+ 9

26	44	27	95	82	55	91
14	17	19	66	27	16	74
+35	+36	+43	+37	+67	+48	+55

306	418	821	752	616	519	803
217	562	159	307	148	425	555
+ 472	+ 334	+ 396	+ 921	+ 272	+395	+ 196

4011	5287	6179	7436	4343
2667	1694	3447	1814	2520
+1884	+3488	+2112	+2067	+8868

8264	9041	7234	5214	1434
1137	5762	1695	1679	8082
+9038	+7730	+2524	+7740	+9848

Math

Name _____

Write the digits in the correct place value order.

Example:

6 thousands	9 hundreds	7 ones	3 hundreds
4 ones	3 tens	5 thousands	9 ones
7 hundreds	8 thousands	2 tens	0 tens
5 tens	1 one	3 hundreds	5 thousands
__6,754__	_____	_____	_____

7 tens	3 thousands	4 hundreds	5 tens
0 hundreds	9 hundreds	0 ones	4 ones
6 thousands	7 ones	9 tens	6 hundreds
1 one	0 tens	6 thousands	2 thousands
_____	_____	_____	_____

Write the value of the circled digit.   **Example:** 9⑥7 2 = 600

7④3 6 = _____   2 0⑥7 = _____   3 6②0 = _____

⑨5 7 2 = _____   4⑨8 1 = _____   ④5 7 6 = _____

1 4 4① = _____   3⑦7 5 = _____   1 8 1④ = _____

5 9④6 = _____   ④2 8 9 = _____   2⑤2 0 = _____

⑧3 9 6 = _____   7 6 5⑨ = _____   7 4⑥6 = _____

Math

Name _____

Work each problem on your calculator. Then, turn the calculator upside down and write the word which should match each clue.

	Answer	Clue	Word
Example: 256 + 362 =	_618_	antonym of small	_Big_
1. 139 + 524 =	_____	a nest occupant	_____
2. 11,862 − 4,757 =	_____	a synonym for dirt	_____
3. 29,331 + 5,675 =	_____	a gander's husband	_____
4. 609 x 5 =	_____	a foot warmer	_____
5. 12,955 − 9,251 =	_____	a gopher's home	_____
6. 323 x 25 =	_____	a messy, unkempt person	_____
7. 9,867 + 25,140 =	_____	an antonym of tight	_____
8. 2,428 ÷ 4 =	_____	fireplace fuel	_____
9. 10,436 − 3,102 =	_____	a foot's back section	_____
10. 918 x 6 =	_____	an employer	_____
11. 3,412 + 4,304 =	_____	a fish uses this to breathe	_____
12. 24,549 ÷ 7 =	_____	an antonym of win	_____
13. 8 x 50 + 9 x 2 =	_____	keeps a baby clean	_____
14. 15 ÷ 3 x 103 =	_____	another name for sister	_____
15. 5 x 60 + 4	_____	gardening tool	_____

Math

Name _____

Add each set of money. Write the total amount on each price tag.

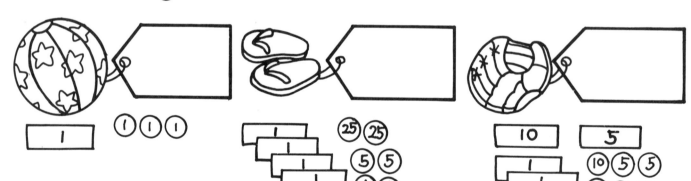

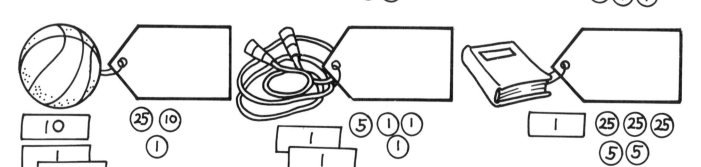

Math

Name _____

Draw the hands on the clock to show the time given.

10:15

7:27

2:04

5:47

11:58

1:11

9:36

3:22

12:13

8:09

4:41

6:18

2:49

10:03

11:31

7:46

Math

Name _____

Read each sentence. Write the number of the matching clock by each sentence.

_____ Peppermint Patty has a gymnastics class at **10:33**.

_____ Freida gets a curly perm at **3:26**.

_____ Charlie Brown's baseball game starts at **11:14**.

_____ Rerun rides on the back of his mom's bike every day at **2:01**.

_____ Schroeder practices the piano at **1:04**.

_____ Marcie gets new glasses at **5:16**.

_____ Linus's blanket has been missing since **6:30**!

_____ Woodstock's flying lessons begin at **9:47**.

_____ Franklin arrives at the party at **7:09**.

_____ Snoopy's suppertime is **5:52**.

_____ Lucy's advice booth opens promptly at **4:39**.

_____ Snoopy's brother, Spike, comes to visit at **8:21**.

Math

Name _____

Work each problem. Then, compare the answers and write the correct sign
(< > =) in the box.

Example:

6 – 4 $\boxed{<}$ 3 + 5   12 – 6 $\square$ 6 + 8   9 + 4 $\square$ 8 + 3

<u> 2 </u>   <u> 8 </u>   ____   ____   ____   ____

15 – 7 $\square$ 4 + 4   7 + 3 $\square$ 11 – 6   3 + 9 $\square$ 6 + 9

____   ____   ____   ____   ____   ____

18 – 9 $\square$ 4 + 5   7 + 7 $\square$ 13 – 5   14 – 6 $\square$ 11 – 4

____   ____   ____   ____   ____   ____

17 – 8 $\square$ 9 + 9   6 + 7 $\square$ 9 + 4   12 – 3 $\square$ 10 – 4

____   ____   ____   ____   ____   ____

5 + 7 $\square$ 8 + 2   15 – 6 $\square$ 3 + 7   16 – 7 $\square$ 8 + 1

____   ____   ____   ____   ____   ____

10 – 1 $\square$ 12 – 4   6 + 5 $\square$ 8 + 4   13 – 4 $\square$ 5 + 3

____   ____   ____   ____   ____   ____

7 + 3 $\square$ 11 – 2   8 – 4 $\square$ 14 – 9   3 + 8 $\square$ 8 + 6

____   ____   ____   ____   ____   ____

Math

Name _____

Work each problem. Then answer the riddle by writing the letter by each problem in the matching numbered blanks below.

(U)
1.   387
    + 596

(M)
2.   495
    + 254

(S)
3.   709
    + 446

(S)
4.   6037
    +6299

(N)
5.   3190
    +5774

(A)
6.   3792
    +7499

(S)
7.   5154
    +2863

(R)
8.   4109
    +2818

(S)
9.   7193
    +1056

(M)
10.   2067
    +1814

(E)
11.   2520
    +1994

(U)
12.   386
      414
    + 592

(E)
13.   746
      223
    + 184

(E)
14.   113
      481
    + 666

(U)
15.   475
      215
    + 986

(G)
16. 4122
     3674
    +5866

(C)
17. 5171
     2441
    +6099

(S)
18. 3749
     2512
    +6631

(L)
19. 5827
     1945
    +7194

What do mathematicians wear to protect their eyes from bright sunshine?

___ ___ ___   ___ ___ ___ ___ ___ ___ ___
 7   12   2   16 19   6   18   3   13   9

Math

Name _____

Work each problem. Then write the letter by each problem in the matching numbered blanks below to complete the sentence.

(U)
1. 317
  −198

(E)
2. 406
  −257

(A)
3. 700
  −351

(E)
4. 824
  −517

(D)
5. 103
  − 77

(S)
6. 115
  − 69

(H)
7. 901
  −452

(N)
8. 625
  −133

(O)
9. 241
  − 37

(E)
10. 733
  −546

(W)
11. 628
  −544

(L)
12. 420
  −175

(Y)
13. 882
  −399

(S)
14. 450
  −263

(T)
15. 505
  −236

(I)
16. 147
  − 89

(S)
17. 902
  −746

(U)
18. 646
  −177

(S)
19. 303
  −196

(I)
20. 132
  − 44

(T)
21. 618
  −419

(V)
22. 700
  −136

(A)
23. 201
  −122

(T)
24. 934
  −555

(T)
25. 821
  −462

(G)
26. 838
  −278

(O)
27. 951
  −374

(Y)
28. 410
  −369

(R)
29. 783
  −255

(H)
30. 411
  −262

Subtraction . . .

__26_ __20_ __22_ __4__ __17_   __28_ __9__ __1__   __12_ __2__ __19_ __6__   __21_ __7__ __3__ __8__

                                                                                            __ __ __ __ __ !

__13_ __27_ __18_   __14_ __25_ __23_ __29_ __15_ __10_ __5__   __11_ __16_ __24_ __30_

Math

Name _____

Work the problems. Remember to put the "$" and "." in each answer. Circle any answer with a "1" in it. Then find the total of all answers with "1"s.

$ 7.46 + 8.25	$13.40 − 9.32	$ 3.58 +9.94	$16.00 − 7.69	$ 4.04 +2.27
$2.14 +8.65	$26.19 − 15.43	$ 7.53 +9.64	$10.01 − 7.17	$12.48 +36.92
$ 5.75 + 1.63	$12.57 − 9.86	$ 9.87 + 4.15	$ 20.67 − 14.81	$ 6.62 + 4.39
$ 2.74 + 9.99	$ 11.32 − 5.66	$ 4.93 + 7.58	$15.00 − 3.34	$ 8.48 + 6.93
$ 5.25 + 1.79	$17.01 − 8.47	$ 6.89 + 7.73	$14.02 − 7.11	$ 5.38 + 8.74

Total _____

Math

Name _____

Wiggle your way from the head of each snake to its tail, by adding and subtracting to reach the final answer.

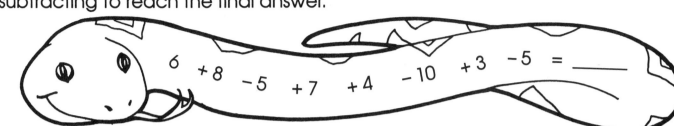

6 +8 −5 +7 +4 −10 +3 −5 = _____

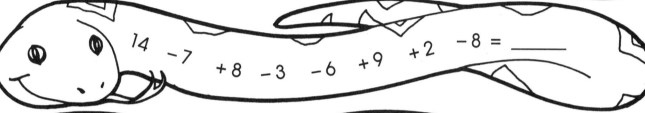

14 −7 +8 −3 −6 +9 +2 −8 = _____

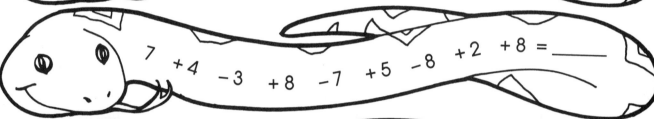

7 +4 −3 +8 −7 +5 −8 +2 +8 = _____

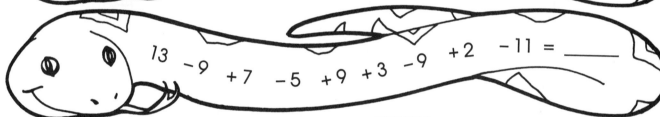

13 −9 +7 −5 +9 +3 −9 +2 −11 = _____

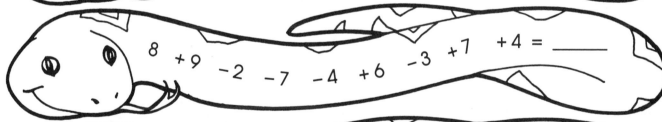

8 +9 −2 −7 −4 +6 −3 +7 +4 = _____

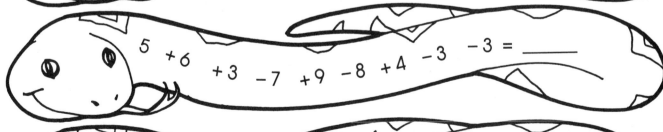

5 +6 +3 −7 +9 −8 +4 −3 −3 = _____

9 +4 −7 +8 −2 +6 −9 +7 −9 = _____

IF8785 Third Grade in Review

Math

Name _____

X 8	Product
7	
4	32

Write each product in the grid as shown.

X 3	Product
4	12
0	
8	
5	
6	
2	
9	

X 8	Product
7	
4	
3	
1	
9	
6	
5	

X 5	Product
2	
9	
4	
7	
8	
6	
0	

X 6	Product
4	
1	
5	
9	
6	
3	
7	

X 9	Product
7	
4	
6	
8	
2	
9	
5	

X 4	Product
9	
4	
7	
5	
6	
3	
2	

X 7	Product
3	
7	
4	
9	
5	
6	
8	

X 2	Product
8	
5	
0	
4	
7	
3	
6	

Bonus:

9 x 8 x 7 x 6 x 5 x 4 x 3 x 2 x 1 x 0 = _____

Math

Name _____

Write each quotient. Then outline the bricks in color according to the color code.

2 = pink	5 = orange	8 = blue
3 = brown	6 = red	9 = purple
4 = yellow	7 = green	1 = black

$16 \div 4 =$ _____ $12 \div 2 =$ _____ $30 \div 6 =$ _____ $4 \div 2 =$ _____

$36 \div 9 =$ _____ $7 \div 7 =$ _____ $21 \div 3 =$ _____

$72 \div 8 =$ _____ $32 \div 4 =$ _____ $56 \div 7 =$ _____

$6 \div 1 =$ _____ $48 \div 6 =$ _____ $9 \div 3 =$ _____

$8 \div 4 =$ _____ $35 \div 7 =$ _____ $18 \div 9 =$ _____

$20 \div 4 =$ _____ $40 \div 5 =$ _____ $36 \div 6 =$ _____ $28 \div 4 =$ _____

$54 \div 6 =$ _____ $12 \div 3 =$ _____ $64 \div 8 =$ _____

$42 \div 6 =$ _____ $24 \div 6 =$ _____ $18 \div 6 =$ _____

$81 \div 9 =$ _____ $4 \div 4 =$ _____ $16 \div 2 =$ _____

$27 \div 9 =$ _____ $48 \div 8 =$ _____ $5 \div 5 =$ _____

$56 \div 8 =$ _____ $14 \div 7 =$ _____

     IF8785 Third Grade in Review

Math

Name _____

Solve each problem.

278 x 3	64 x 8	345 x 5	82 x 7	894 x 4
159 x 6	88 x 3	791 x 4	56 x 6	587 x 7
309 x 9	47 x 4	617 x 4	73 x 9	215 x 6
410 x 6	39 x 7	455 x 8	94 x 8	308 x 6
752 x 6	77 x 3	862 x 7	48 x 8	754 x 7

Circle the mystery problem. It has a 4-digit answer which counts by 2's from left to right.

Math

Name _____

Watch out for remainders as you divide these problems.

Example:

$$4\overline{)27}\text{6 R. 3}$$
$$\underline{24}$$
$$3$$

$6\overline{)40}$ $3\overline{)13}$ $7\overline{)50}$

$8\overline{)44}$ $9\overline{)17}$ $5\overline{)19}$ $6\overline{)21}$

$4\overline{)35}$ $2\overline{)9}$ $3\overline{)29}$ $9\overline{)57}$

$6\overline{)52}$ $7\overline{)24}$ $8\overline{)35}$ $4\overline{)17}$

$3\overline{)17}$ $2\overline{)11}$ $6\overline{)56}$ $7\overline{)60}$

$4\overline{)23}$ $9\overline{)12}$ $5\overline{)41}$ $8\overline{)26}$

Math

Name _____

Color each fractional part.

Example:
Color ⅗ blue.

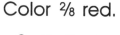

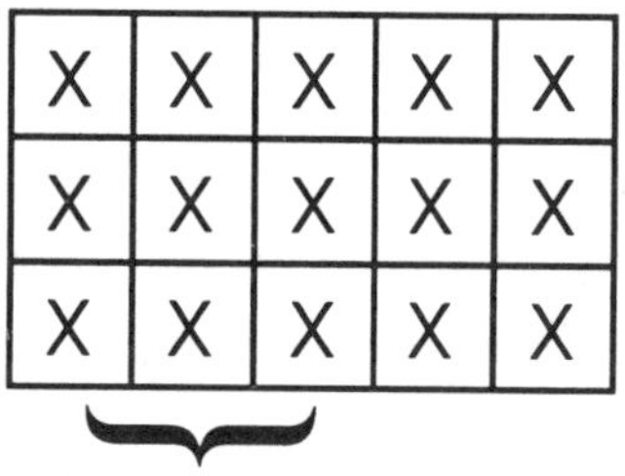

⅗ of 15 = _9_

½ of 2 = 🦴

Color ¾ orange.

¾ of 12 = ____

Color ⅜ red.

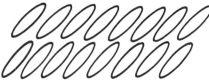

⅜ of 16 = ____

Color 3/6 green.

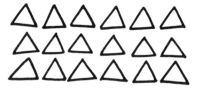

3/6 of 18 = ____

Color ½ brown.

½ of 8 = ____

Color ⅘ purple.

⅘ of 20 = ____

Color ⅓ blue.

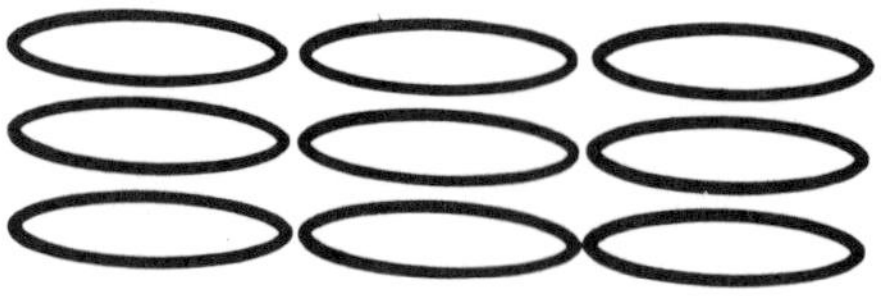

⅓ of 9 = ____

Color 2/4 yellow.

2/4 of 16 = ____

Color ⅓ pink.

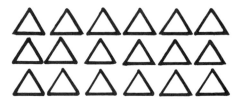

⅓ of 18 = ____

Color ⅜ red.

⅜ of 24 = ____

Color ⅕ green.

⅕ of 10 = ____

Color 4/7 orange.

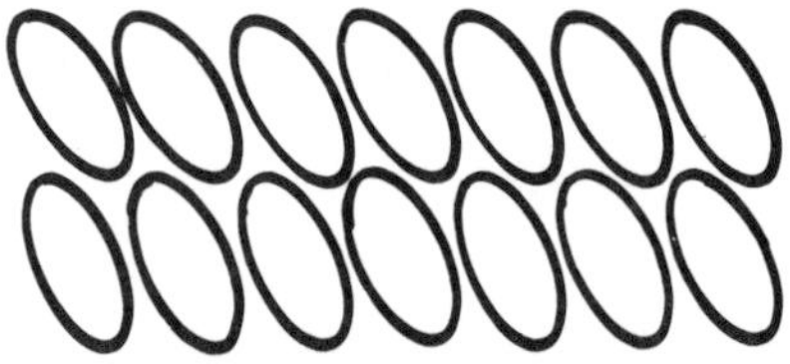

4/7 of 14 = ____

Color ⅔ yellow.

⅔ of 21 = ____

IF8785 Third Grade in Review

Math

Name _____

Create each object using the geometric shapes indicated.

circle   triangle   rectangle   trapezoid   cylinder   cone   square

Robot	House	Boat
1 cy, 4 r, 1 co, 3 t, 1 c	2 r, 1 t, 3 s	3 t, 2 c, 1 r, 1 tr
Lighthouse	**Fence**	**Scarecrow**
1 cy, 1 co, 1 c, 4 s	4 r, 4 t	1 tr, 2 r, 2 cy, 1 s

Use as many shapes as you can to design a city.

Math

Name _____

P = 2+2+1+1+1+3 = 10   A = 5

Perimeter is the distance around an area. **Area** is the space inside a shape. Find the perimeter and area for each shape using each square unit.

Example:

P = _20_ units

A = _18_ sq. units

P = ____ units

A = ____ sq. units

P = ____ units

A = ____ sq. units

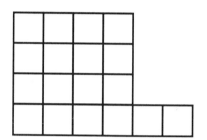 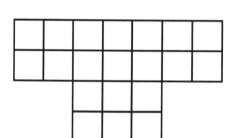 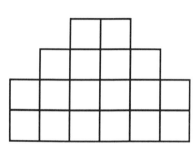

P = ____ units

A = ____ sq. units

P = ____ units

A = ____ sq. units

P = ____ units

A = ____ sq. units

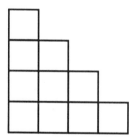 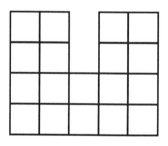 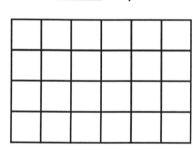

P = ____ units

A = ____ sq. units

P = ____ units

A = ____ sq. units

P = ____ units

A = ____ sq. units

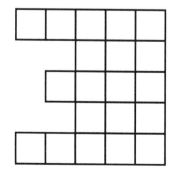 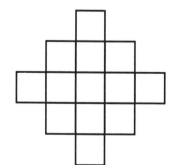 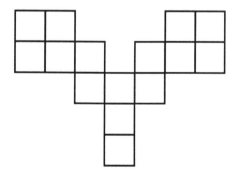

IF8785 Third Grade in Review

Math

Name _____

Place **+, −, x**, or **÷** in each box to complete each number sentence.

4 ☐ 5 = 20	9 ☐ 7 = 16	9 ☐ 8 = 17
7 ☐ 7 = 0	4 ☐ 1 = 3	30 ☐ 6 = 5
8 ☐ 6 = 14	9 ☐ 2 = 11	9 ☐ 2 = 18
81 ☐ 9 = 9	16 ☐ 8 = 2	12 ☐ 4 = 8
13 ☐ 5 = 8	32 ☐ 4 = 8	54 ☐ 6 = 9
6 ☐ 6 = 36	3 ☐ 6 = 18	8 ☐ 8 = 64
9 ☐ 0 = 0	13 ☐ 4 = 9	5 ☐ 1 = 6
7 ☐ 6 = 13	7 ☐ 2 = 9	12 ☐ 10 = 2
36 ☐ 4 = 9	20 ☐ 4 = 5	6 ☐ 4 = 24
11 ☐ 6 = 5	5 ☐ 5 = 25	48 ☐ 8 = 6
8 ☐ 7 = 56	17 ☐ 9 = 8	2 ☐ 8 = 10
14 ☐ 7 = 7	72 ☐ 8 = 9	3 ☐ 5 = 15
9 ☐ 3 = 3	3 ☐ 4 = 12	42 ☐ 6 = 7
7 ☐ 4 = 28	2 ☐ 2 = 4	7 ☐ 1 = 6
5 ☐ 7 = 12	40 ☐ 5 = 8	8 ☐ 3 = 24
10 ☐ 6 = 4	7 ☐ 7 = 49	8 ☐ 8 = 16
16 ☐ 4 = 4	10 ☐ 3 = 7	3 ☐ 9 = 12
3 ☐ 7 = 21	6 ☐ 2 = 4	10 ☐ 5 = 2

Math

Name _____

Use the pictograph about pets to answer the questions below.

Perky Pets (Each picture = 2 animals)

Fish	🐟 🐟 🐟
Cats	🐱 🐱 🐱 🐱 🐱 🐱
Gerbils	🐹 🐹
Dogs	🐕 🐕 🐕 🐕 🐕 🐕 🐕
Hamsters	🐹 🐹
Turtles	🐢 🐢
Birds	🐦 🐦 🐦
Horses	🐎 🐎 🐎 🐎 🐎

1. Write a number sentence to show the total number of dogs and cats.

   _____

2. There are six of which animals? _____

3. There are the least of which three animals? _____

4. How many more dogs than horses are there? _____

5. How many footless animals are shown? _____

6. What is the total number of horses, cats, turtles, and birds shown? _____

7. How many animal's names begin with the letter **H**? _____

8. There are the most of which animals? _____

9. How many more dogs than fish are there? _____

10. What is the total number of animals shown on the pictograph? _____

Math

Name _____

Use the information given to fill in one vertical and one horizontal bar graph.

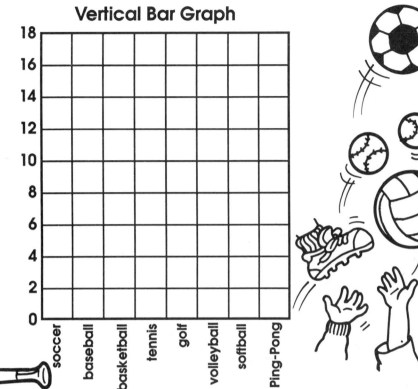

Vertical Bar Graph

Plot these sports balls on the graph.

- 6 soccer balls
- 14 basketballs
- 10 golf balls
- 8 softballs
- 16 baseballs
- 4 tennis balls
- 12 volleyballs
- 2 Ping-Pong balls

Now, chart these pieces of sports equipment on the horizontal bar graph.

| 7 golf clubs | 11 bats | 9 batting gloves | 8 catcher's mitts |
| 4 knee pads | 2 nets | 16 golf tees | 18 racquets |

Horizontal Bar Graph

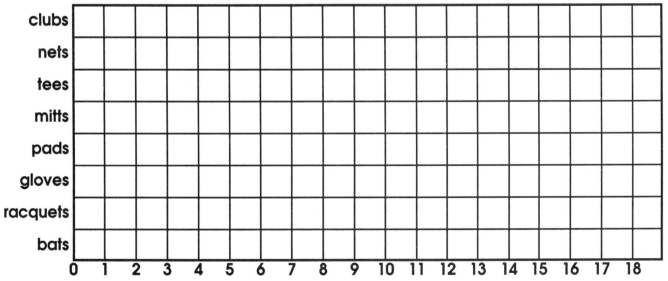

63

Math

Name _____

Use the line graph to answer the questions.

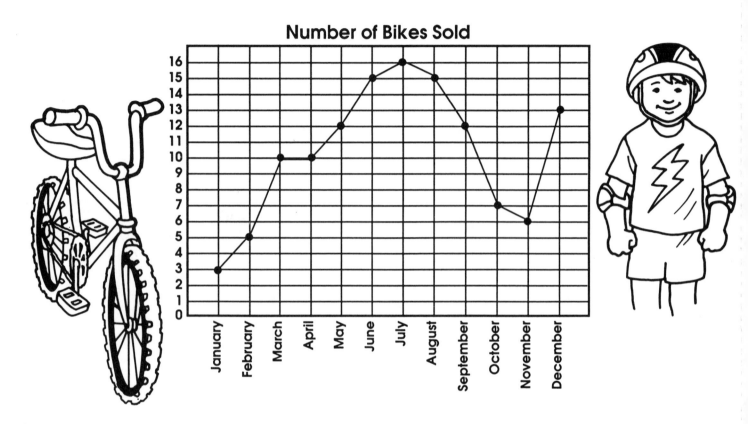

1. In which month were the most bikes sold? _____

2. What is the total number of bikes sold in March and April? _____

3. What is the difference between the number of bikes sold in July and those sold in October? _____

4. In which 2 months were 15 bikes sold? _____

5. In which 3 months were less than 7 sold? _____

6. In which 2 months were 12 bikes sold? _____

7. What is the total of bikes sold in October, November, and December? _____

8. In June, July, and August, how many total bikes were sold? _____

9. In which months were more than 12 sold? _____

10. How many bikes were sold in the entire year? _____

Math

Name _____

Complete the multiplication grid by writing the products in the boxes.

X	4	9	0	3	8	5	1	7	2	6
2										
8				24						
1										
6								42		
7										
4					32					
0										
9										
5										
3										

Write the product for each problem.

6	5	6	4	5	4
x 8	x 4	x 5	x 7	x 3	x 4

7	8	9	6	7	8
x 6	x 3	x 2	x 4	x 3	x 4

9	3	6	7	8	4
x 5	x 4	x 6	x 5	x 6	x 5

IF8785 Third Grade in Review

Math

Name _____

A magic square contains numbers that add up to the same sum, across, down, and diagonally. Fill in the numbers to make these magic squares.

	3	
1	5	9
	7	

Fill in 8, 2, 6, and 4.

The magic sum is _____ .

6		10
11		
4		8

Fill in 3, 5, 9, and 7.

The magic sum is _____ .

	2	
6	10	14
		4

Fill in 16, 12, 8, and 18.

The magic sum is _____ .

11		13
12	10	
	14	

Fill in 9, 8, 7, and 6.

The magic sum is _____ .

	1	6
	5	7
	9	

Fill in 2, 3, 4, and 8.

The magic sum is _____ .

12	7	
		9
8	15	

Fill in 13, 14, 10, and 11.

The magic sum is _____ .

Social Studies

Name _____

Use the compass rose to write directions for each set of arrows. Begin at the ★.

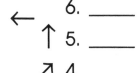

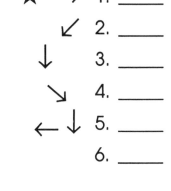

6. ____
5. ____
4. ____
3. ____
2. ____
1. ____

6. ____
5. ____
4. ____
3. ____
2. ____
1. ____

1. ____
2. ____
3. ____
4. ____
5. ____
6. ____

6. ____
5. ____
4. ____
3. ____
2. ____
1. ____

1. ____
2. ____
3. ____
4. ____
5. ____

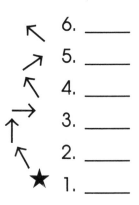

6. ____
5. ____
4. ____
3. ____
2. ____
1. ____

Now it's your turn! Start at the stars to draw the arrow patterns for these directions.

1. S ★
2. E
3. S
4. E
5. S
6. E

6. E
5. N
4. W
3. N
2. NE
1. NE ★

1. SW ★
2. SW
3. E
4. S
5. E
6. NE

IF8785 Third Grade in Review

Social Studies

Name _____

Write the capital of each state by putting one letter in each section of the caterpillar. The last letter of each word will be the first letter of the next word.

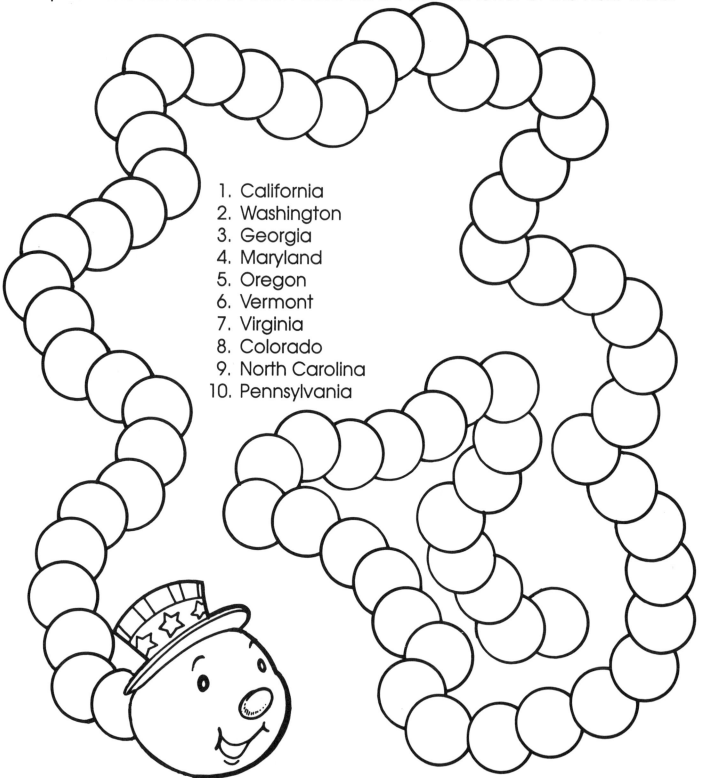

1. California
2. Washington
3. Georgia
4. Maryland
5. Oregon
6. Vermont
7. Virginia
8. Colorado
9. North Carolina
10. Pennsylvania

Social Studies

Name _____

Label the continents and oceans of the four hemispheres.

Western Hemisphere

1. _North America_
2. _____
3. _____
4. _____

Eastern Hemisphere

1. _____
2. _____
3. _____
4. _____
5. _____
6. _____
7. _____

Southern Hemisphere

1. _____
2. _____
3. _____
4. _____
5. _____
6. _____
7. _____

Northern Hemisphere

1. _____
2. _____
3. _____
4. _____
5. _____
6. _____
7. _____

Social Studies

Name _____

Follow the directions below to complete the globe.

1. Draw a red line for the equator.

2. Draw a green dotted line for the prime meridian.

3. Put a purple **X** for the North Pole.

4. Put a brown **X** for the South Pole.

5. Draw four yellow lines of longitude, connecting at the North and South Poles.

6. Draw eight orange lines of latitude spaced evenly apart.

7. Name the four hemispheres. _____ _____

   _____ _____

8. In which two hemispheres do you live? _____

   _____

Social Studies

Name _____

Create a map on the grid by following the directions below.

	1	2	3	4	5	6	7
A							
B							
C							
D							
E							
F							

1. Draw a lake covering boxes E5, E6, F5, and F6.

2. Put evergreen trees in E7 and F7.

3. Draw a pier at E4.

4. Put canoes at D6 and F4.

5. Add tour buses at E2 and E3.

6. Draw a lodge covering F2 and F3.

7. Draw a "Welcome to Camp" sign at F1.

8. Draw a flower garden covering D1, D2, D3, and E1.

9. Draw sailboats at D5, D7, and C6.

10. Draw a diagonal path cutting through D4, C5, B6, and A7.

11. Put tents at C4, A5, A6, B5, B7, and C7.

12. Draw a bear at B3.

13. Draw a raccoon in C1.

14. Draw a forest covering A1, A2, B1, B2, C2, and C3.

15. Draw birds in A3, A4, and B4.

Social Studies

Name _____

The letters and numbers on the grid are called coordinates. Use the coordinates to find who's who at the zoo.

1. The elephants are found in _____, _____ , _____

2. What would you do at A3 and A4? _____

3. Where are the monkeys? _____ , _____, _____

4. What would you see at A5 and B5? _____

5. Where is the gorilla? _____

6. To what animal family do those in A6, A7, B6, and B7 belong? _____

7. Where would you find kangaroos? _____

8. Where could you picnic? _____ , _____ , _____ , _____

9. What would you see at C2? _____

10. Where would you see snakes? _____ , _____ , _____

11. Lizards are found at _____

12. What would you see at C1? _____

13. Where would you go to see water animals? _____ , _____ , _____

14. What is at E3? _____

15. Bears could be found at _____ , _____ , _____ , _____

16. Where are the giraffes? _____

IF8785 Third Grade in Review

Social Studies

Name _____

Use the latitude and longitude coordinates to answer each question.

1. What line of longitude passes through the middle of the waterslide? _____

2. The roller coaster goes between what lines of latitude? _____

3. The carousel crosses which longitude line? _____

4. To go from the pop stand to the cotton candy, which longitude lines do you cross? _____

5. From the Pirate's Ship to the Dodge 'Em Cars, you pass which lines of latitude? _____

6. The sand dunes lie between which lines of longitude? _____

7. The kiddie rides are between _____ and _____ latitude and _____ and _____ longitude.

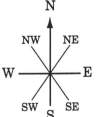

8. From the beach to the sand dunes, you cross what latitude line? _____

9. If you cross 40°N from the hot dog stand, where are you? _____

10. The nachos are between _____ and _____ latitude, and _____ and _____ longitude.

11. Which line of longitude passes through the center of the Log Ride? _____

12. Which longitude line do you pass to go from the entrance gate to the ticket booth ? _____

Social Studies

Name _____

Follow the directions to complete the United States map on page 75.

1. Draw blue lines to show the Mississippi, Ohio, Missouri, Colorado, and Red rivers.

2. Color the five Great Lakes blue.

3. Put a red ☆ on Washington, D.C.

4. Draw brown ⛰ for the Appalachian and the Rocky Mountains.

5. Color the Hawaiian Islands green.

6. Draw blue and white vertical stripes on Alaska.

7. Color every state whose name has two words in it purple.

8. Draw a yellow smiling face on your home state.

9. Draw four orange fish in the Gulf of Mexico.

10. Put an orange △ on the largest contiguous state.

11. Color the state first in ABC order yellow.

12. Color the state last in ABC order with green polka dots.

13. Draw brown **X**'s along the southern U.S. border.

14. Draw red dots on all states that start with "**I**."

15. Draw blue 〜 on the Great Salt Lake.

16. Draw pink stripes on the state whose name has only one syllable.

Social Studies

Name _____

Use with page 74.

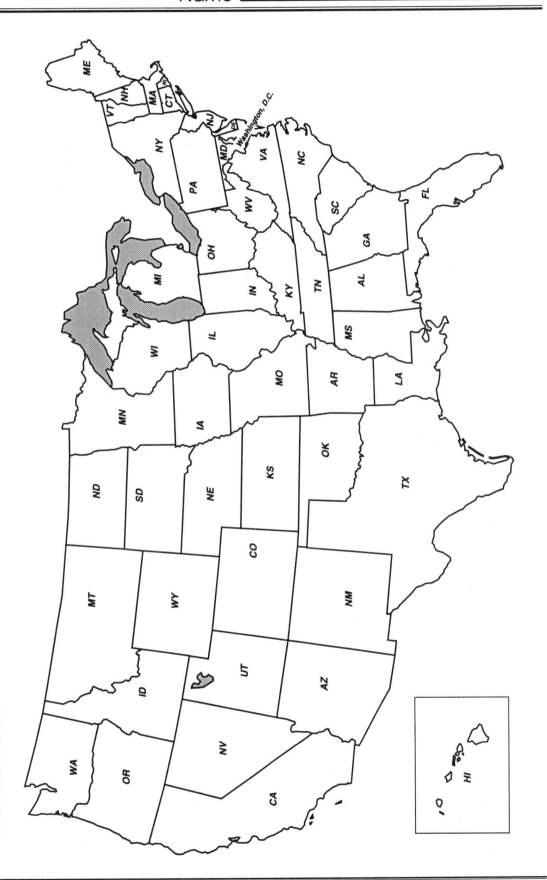

Social Studies

Name _____

Follow the directions to create a banner of our national symbols.

1. Draw a bald eagle in the northwest corner.

2. Draw a soldier to represent Yankee Doodle in the southeast corner.

3. Draw Uncle Sam in the middle.

4. Draw the Statue of Liberty in the northeast corner.

5. Draw the Capitol building in the southwest corner.

6. Draw the Liberty Bell below Uncle Sam.

7. Draw our nation's flag above Uncle Sam.

8. Below the eagle, draw three musical notes—one red, one white, and one blue— to represent the Star Spangled Banner.

9. Above Yankee Doodle, draw a boat to represent the Boston Tea Party.

Social Studies

Name _____

Write the number of each Washington, D.C. attraction in the box by its picture.
Choose two attractions to write a report on.

1. Lincoln Memorial
2. Vietnam Veterans Memorial
3. Washington Monument
4. Supreme Court Building
5. United States Capitol
6. White House

7. Arlington National Cemetery
8. Jefferson Memorial
9. Museum of Natural History
10. The Marine Corps War Memorial
11. Ford's Theater
12. Air and Space Museum

IF8785 Third Grade in Review

Social Studies

Name _____

Write the name of each state next to its two-letter abbreviation.

1. CT _____	26. IL _____	
2. DE _____	27. IN _____	
3. AK _____	28. IA _____	
4. ME _____	29. MI _____	
5. MD _____	30. MN _____	
6. MA _____	31. MO _____	
7. NH _____	32. OH _____	
8. NJ _____	33. WI _____	
9. NY _____	34. KS _____	
10. PA _____	35. NE _____	
11. RI _____	36. ND _____	
12. VT _____	37. OK _____	
13. WV _____	38. SD _____	
14. AL _____	39. TX _____	
15. AR _____	40. AZ _____	
16. FL _____	41. CA _____	
17. GA _____	42. CO _____	
18. KY _____	43. ID _____	
19. HI _____	44. MT _____	
20. LA _____	45. NV _____	
21. MS _____	46. NM _____	
22. NC _____	47. OR _____	
23. SC _____	48. UT _____	
24. TN _____	49. WA _____	
25. VA _____	50. WY _____	

Social Studies

Name _____

Unscramble the names of these physical features found in our country. Then use the numbers to label the map below.

1. n a i l d s _____

2. u t i m o a n n _____

3. s p a l n n i e u _____

4. a p l i n _____

5. c a n o e _____

6. d r o b e r _____

7. f u l g _____

8. v i r e r _____

9. e l k a _____

10. t a c o s _____

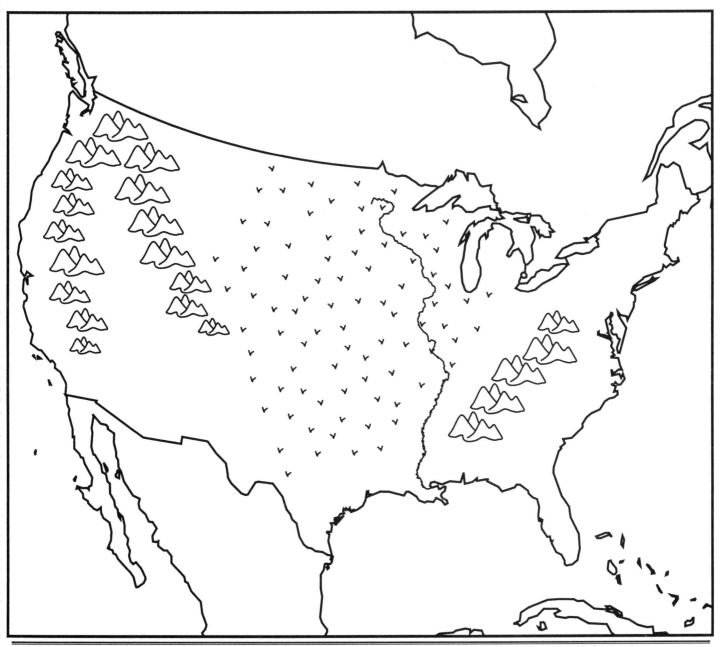

Social Studies

Name _____

Arrange the dates in the correct order to construct the transportation time line below. Write only the year and the underlined key word(s) on the time line.

1919—First commercial <u>airline</u> began service.

1830—First steam <u>locomotive</u> on the B&O Railroad.

1903—Wright brothers' first successful <u>airplane</u> flight.

1807—First successful U.S.A. <u>steamboat</u> service began.

1969—First rocket flight to the <u>moon</u> by the U.S.

1825—Opening of the Erie <u>Canal</u>.

1893—First successful American gasoline-powered <u>automobile</u> built.

1897—First American <u>subway</u> opened in Boston.

1869—First <u>railroad</u> line crossing the U.S. completed.

1981—First <u>space shuttle</u> flight.

• Transportation Time Line •

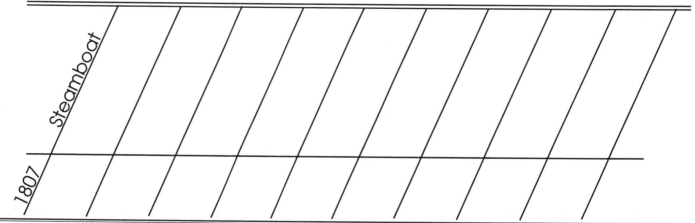

Social Studies

Name _____

Number the events telling of the history of U.S. communication in order. Then illustrate each one in the correct box.

_____ In 1953, color telecasts began.

_____ The first public subscription library in the U.S. was founded in 1731.

_____ Samuel Morse first publicly demonstrated the telegraph in 1837.

_____ The U.S. began regular TV broadcasts in 1939.

_____ In 1741, the first magazine was published in the U.S.

_____ Alexander Graham Bell patented the first successful telephone in 1876.

_____ In 1833, the first successful penny newspaper was published in New York.

_____ The first regular radio broadcasts began in 1920.

3	6	1	7
4	8	2	5

Social Studies

Name _____

Read each clue. Circle the name of the corresponding holiday in the wordsearch. Use the color given.

1. Honors our first president   (purple)
2. Celebrates the discovery of our country   (green)
3. Our country's birthday—July 4, 1776   (blue)
4. Honors the banner of the U.S.   (red)
5. A holiday to give thanks   (orange)
6. Honors those who died in past wars   (black)
7. Remembers the president who put an end to slavery   (yellow)
8. Remembers the man who fought peacefully for civil rights   (pink)
9. Honors our country's workers   (brown)

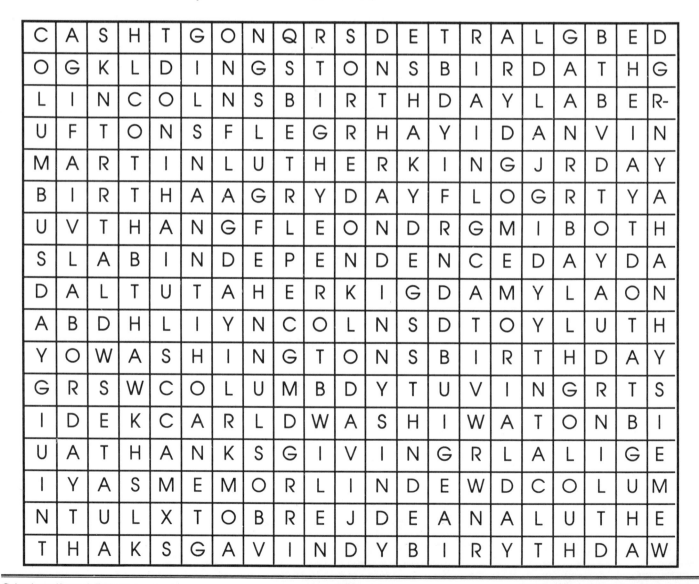

C	A	S	H	T	G	O	N	Q	R	S	D	E	T	R	A	L	G	B	E	D
O	G	K	L	D	I	N	G	S	T	O	N	S	B	I	R	D	A	T	H	G
L	I	N	C	O	L	N	S	B	I	R	T	H	D	A	Y	L	A	B	E	R-
U	F	T	O	N	S	F	L	E	G	R	H	A	Y	I	D	A	N	V	I	N
M	A	R	T	I	N	L	U	T	H	E	R	K	I	N	G	J	R	D	A	Y
B	I	R	T	H	A	A	G	R	Y	D	A	Y	F	L	O	G	R	T	Y	A
U	V	T	H	A	N	G	F	L	E	O	N	D	R	G	M	I	B	O	T	H
S	L	A	B	I	N	D	E	P	E	N	D	E	N	C	E	D	A	Y	D	A
D	A	L	T	U	T	A	H	E	R	K	I	G	D	A	M	Y	L	A	O	N
A	B	D	H	L	I	Y	N	C	O	L	N	S	D	T	O	Y	L	U	T	H
Y	O	W	A	S	H	I	N	G	T	O	N	S	B	I	R	T	H	D	A	Y
G	R	S	W	C	O	L	U	M	B	D	Y	T	U	V	I	N	G	R	T	S
I	D	E	K	C	A	R	L	D	W	A	S	H	I	W	A	T	O	N	B	I
U	A	T	H	A	N	K	S	G	I	V	I	N	G	R	L	A	L	I	G	E
I	Y	A	S	M	E	M	O	R	L	I	N	D	E	W	D	C	O	L	U	M
N	T	U	L	X	T	O	B	R	E	J	D	E	A	N	A	L	U	T	H	E
T	H	A	K	S	G	A	V	I	N	D	Y	B	I	R	Y	T	H	D	A	W

Science

Name _____

Plants and animals are living things called organisms. They have five features in common. Unscramble the sentences to identify these features.

1. to must they able grow be

   _____

2. cells of made are they more or one

   _____

3. need they food

   _____

4. their environment to they respond

   _____

5. can reproduce they

   _____

Color only the pictures of the things with the five features.

Science

Name _____

All organisms pass through life cycles with varying numbers of stages. The monarch butterfly has four stages in its life cycle. Unscramble each word to identify the stages.

Stage 1: g e g _____

Laid on plants, some are smaller than a pinhead

Stage 2: l i a r c e ta p r l

_____

Most are green or brown, last at least two weeks, shed skin 4-5 times

Stage 3: a p p u _____

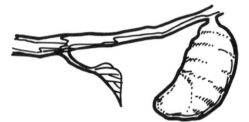

Shell that forms around the caterpillar and hardens

Stage 4: t d l u a f u t r e l b y t

_____

Emerges from pupa, lives from a week or two to 18 months

Now draw **your** life cycle—past, present, and future.

Baby	**Toddler**	**Child**	**Teenager**	**Adult**

Science

Name _____

Place the animals listed below in the correct family by writing their names on the lines.

Fish

_____

_____

_____

Amphibians

_____

_____

_____

Insects

_____

_____

_____

Reptiles

_____

_____

_____

Birds

_____

_____

_____

Mammals

_____

_____

_____

alligator	trout	rattlesnake	flamingo	raccoon
perch	whale	ladybug	salmon	newt
parrot	robin	crocodile	dragonfly	shark
horse	dog	salamander	lizard	penguin
cobra	frog	grasshopper	peacock	beetle

Science

Name _____

A habitat is an animal's home. Choose an animal from the Word Bank that might live in each habitat.

Word Bank

whale
pig
barnacle
frog
penguin
bee
ant
rattlesnake
monkey
buffalo
bear
bird

Science

Name _____

Endangered animals are those which may not survive. Extinct animals are no longer living. Use the code to identify these endangered or extinct animals.

A	B	C	D	E	F	G	H	I	J	K	L	M
3	17	8	11	1	23	14	19	4	26	21	13	7
N	O	P	Q	R	S	T	U	V	W	X	Y	Z
9	2	15	20	10	6	12	5	18	24	22	16	25

Endangered Animals

1. 17–3–13–11   1–3–14–13–1 _____

2. 10–1–11   24–2–13–23 _____

3. 23–13–2–10–4–11–3   15–3–9–12–19–1–10 _____

4. 24–2–2–11   17–4–6–2–9 _____

5. 7–4–6–6–4–2–9   17–13–5–1   17–5–12–12–1–10–23–13–16

   _____

6. 8–3–13–4–23–2–10–9–4–3   8–2–9–11–2–10 _____

7. 6–12–1–13–13–1–10–6   6–1–3   13–4–2–9 _____

8. 2–8–1–13–2–12 _____

9. 14–10–4–25–25–13–16   17–1–3–10 _____

10. 24–19–2–2–15–4–9–14   8–10–3–9–1 _____

Extinct Animals

1. 11–4–9–2–6–3–5–10 _____

2. 7–2–3 _____

3. 15–3–6–6–1–9–14–1–10   15–4–14–1–2–9 _____

4. 6–12–1–13–13–1–10–6   6–1–3   8–2–24 _____

5. 24–2–2–13–13–16   7–3–7–7–2–12–19 _____

6. 13–3–17–10–3–11–2–10   11–5–8–21 _____

7. 11–2–11–2   17–4–10–11 _____

8. 14–10–1–3–12   3–5–21 _____

Science

Name _____

Many plants grow from seeds. Label the seed parts—developing plant, stored food, and seed coat.

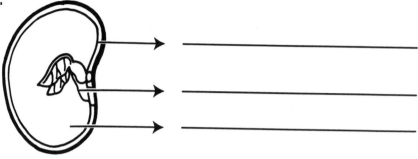

_____

_____

_____

Seeds come in many sizes and shapes. Write the seed's name under each picture.

maple seed	milkweed	corn
coconut	lima bean	wheat
dandelion	strawberry	acorn

IF8785 Third Grade in Review

Science

Name _____

Plants give us many things we need. Follow the numbers to write some things plants give us.

1. 10 6 5 1 2 7 8 4 3 9
    s a t v e b l e g e

6. 4 2 6 5 3 1
    b u r e b r

2. 6 5 4 2 1 3
   r e b u l m

7. 4 5 2 1 6 3
   g e x o n y

3. 4 2 5 6 1 3
   i r t s f u

8. 3 2 4 5 1   5 4 3 1 2
   p a l e m   p u r s y

4. 4 2 1 5 3 6
   t o c o t n

9. 2 5 1 3 4
   i n l n e

5. 2 1 4 3 5
   a p e p r

10. 4 3 2 5 1 6
    c i p e s s

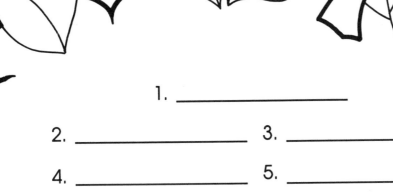

1. _____

2. _____ 3. _____

4. _____ 5. _____

6. _____ 7. _____

8. _____ 9. _____

10. _____

IF8785 Third Grade in Review

Science

Name _____

There are many kinds of energy. Use the key to mark the kind of energy each object produces.

H = heat	S = sound	M = motion
L = light	E = electricity	

____ 1. a battery

____ 2. coal

____ 3. power drill

____ 4. flashlight

____ 5. toaster

____ 6. campfire

____ 7. vibrating drum

____ 8. toy train

____ 9. violin

____ 10. lasers

____ 11. vocal cords

____ 12. hair dryer

Science

Name _____

Use the weather words from the Weather Bank to work the puzzle.

Weather Bank

predict	thermometer	dew	windy
cloud	smog	blizzard	thunder
icicle	hurricane	tornado	snow
precipitation	frost	rain	sleet

Across:

2. to foretell upcoming weather
3. used to measure temperature
5. frozen water vapor
6. a collection of water droplets high in the air
8. a heavy, windy, blinding snowstorm
9. needlelike frozen water
10. a windy funnel-shaped storm
11. water vapor condensing on a cool object
12. breezy
13. liquid precipitation
14. solid, flaky precipitation

Down:

1. smoke and fog
2. water that falls to earth
4. a storm that forms over an ocean
7. partially frozen rain
10. the sound that follows lightning

IF8785 Third Grade in Review

Science

Name _____

Write the name of the correct planet by each clue.

Pluto	Venus	Saturn
Neptune	Uranus	Mercury
Earth	Jupiter	Mars

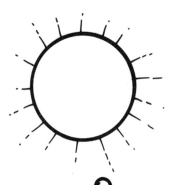

_____ 1. The hottest planet

_____ 2. Has a giant red spot

_____ 3. The largest planet

_____ 4. Has rings and 15 moons

_____ 5. The smallest planet

_____ 6. Has living organisms

_____ 7. The second largest planet

_____ 8. It has 18 moons and seven rings

_____ 9. About 70% water

_____ 10. Has giant volcanoes

_____ 11. Has eight moons, only two of which can be seen
from Earth's telescopes.

_____ 12. A reddish planet with 2 moons

_____ 13. Has water, clouds, and atmosphere

_____ 14. It's about the same size as Uranus

_____ 15. It is 93 million miles from the sun

_____ 16. Its orbit crosses Pluto's every 248 years

_____ 17. Covered with thick, poisonous clouds

_____ 18. Closest to the sun, no moons

Write the names of the nine planets in order from the sun.

1. _____   4. _____   7. _____

2. _____   5. _____   8. _____

3. _____   6. _____   9. _____

Science

Name _____

Create a car of the future by combining these simple machines. Use at least one of each kind. Name your new model.

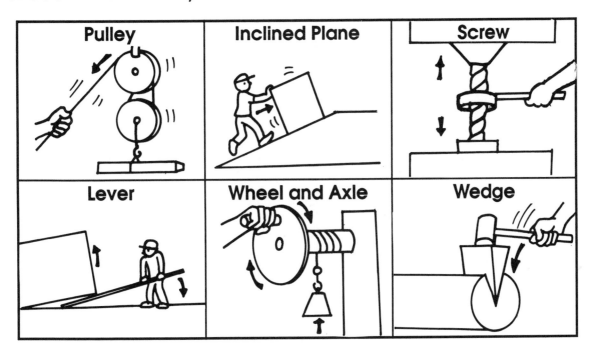

| Pulley | Inclined Plane | Screw |
| Lever | Wheel and Axle | Wedge |

Car of the Future

Model Name _____

Science

Name _____

Read each clue and then write the matching scientist on the line.

1. I study the stars and other celestial bodies. _____	6. I study the effects of electricity. _____
2. I work with chemical combinations. _____	7. I help preserve animals' habitats. _____
3. I am a space traveler. _____	8. I study all forms of animal life. _____
4. I study the earth's physical features. _____	9. I study fossil remains. _____
5. I study and predict the weather. _____	10. I study plant life. _____

Word Bank

chemist   electrical engineer   astronaut
astronomer   meteorologist   conservationist
zoologist   paleontologist   geologist
botanist

Health

Name _____

Draw the number of servings needed daily from each food group.

fats, sweets, oils

milk, yogurt, cheese

meats, poultry, fish, eggs, nuts, dry beans

vegetables

fruits

breads, cereal, rice, pasta

LUNCH

Health

Name _____

Decorate this checkered tablecloth. Decide the food group to which each of these foods belongs. Color according to the pyramid key to the right.

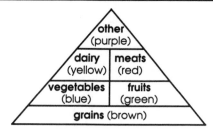

potato	turkey	cake	onion	milk	pickle
peach	eggs	watermelon	bologna	apple	carrot
hot dog	beet	yogurt	grapes	hamburger	bun
bread	ham	cucumber	cheddar cheese	brownie	peanuts
chicken	candy bar	bagel	lettuce	steak	banana
cherry	walnuts	bacon	pineapple	orange	sour cream
cream cheese	lima beans	crackers	ice cream	corn	rice
macaroni	pork chop	cabbage	biscuits	lemon	butter
spinach	donut	nectarine	ham	plum	strawberry
green beans	pecans	cream	spaghetti	Popsicle™	veal

Health

Name _____

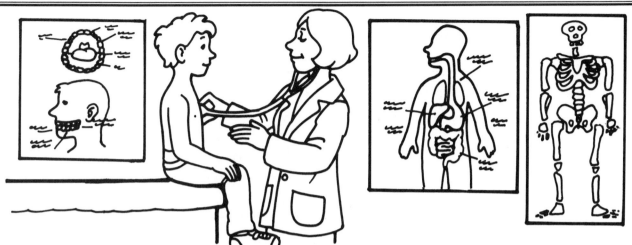

Your body is an amazing machine with many parts. Write the correct word from the Word Bank in each blank.

Word Bank		
enamel	fingerprint	bones
hairs	nerve fibers	colors
water	blood vessels	beats
skin	muscles	

1. Half of the 200 _____ in your body are in your hands and feet.

2. _____ make up half of the weight of your body.

3. _____ is the largest organ in the human body.

4. Tooth _____ is the hardest substance in your body.

5. Messages travel along your _____ at 3 to 300 feet per second.

6. Your eyes can distinguish more than 200 _____ .

7. Your heart _____ about 36 million times a year.

8. An average person has 100,000 _____ on his head.

9. The body is made of about 65% _____ .

10. Your _____ could branch out 60,000 miles.

11. No two people have the same pattern of loops, whorls, or arches in their

   _____ .

Health

Name _____

Show what you know about teeth. Label each box using words from the Word Bank.

Word Bank

cavity	pulp	toothpaste
floss	crown	calcium
plaque	root	primary teeth
gums	enamel	permanent teeth

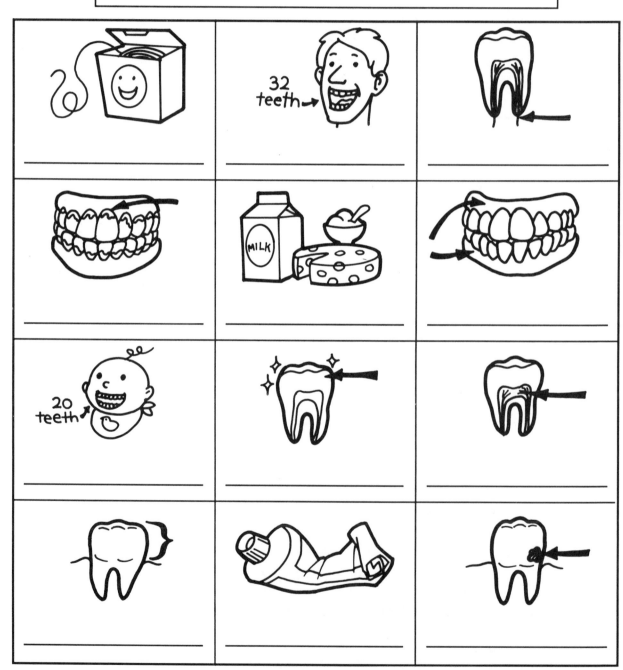

Health

Name _____

In an emergency, you need to know what to do to help. Use the code to complete these important first aid rules.

A–1	G–7	L–12	Q–17	V–22
B–2	H–8	M–13	R–18	W–23
C–3	I–9	N–14	S–19	X–24
D–4	J–10	O–15	T–20	Y–25
E–5	K–11	P–16	U–21	Z–26
F–6				

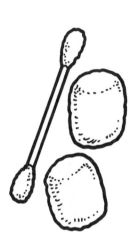

Rules:

1. Stay 3–1–12–13! _____

2. Cover someone who is in 19–8–15–3–11. _____

3. Get an 1–4–21–12–20 to help you. _____

4. 3–1–12–12 the emergency number 911. _____

5. Make sure the 911 operator gets all the 9–14–6–15–18–13–1–20–9–15–14.

   _____

6. Do not move an 9–14–10–21–18–5–4 person. _____

7. Tell the injured person where you are going if you leave to get 8–5–12–16.

   _____

8. Press a clean 3–12–15–20–8 over a bad cut. _____

9. A bleeding body part should be held 8–9–7–8–5–18 than the level of the

   heart. _____

 IF8785 Third Grade in Review

Health

Name _____

A well-groomed person has a neat and clean appearance. Try keeping this grooming chart for one week. Place a ☺ for each well-done task, a 😐 for a task done but not well, and a ☹ for one not done or done poorly. After one week, evaluate your chart and work on your weaker areas.

Task	Sunday	Monday	Tuesday	Wednes-day	Thursday	Friday	Saturday
1. shower or bathe							
2. wear clean clothes							
3. brush teeth 3 times a day							
4. sleep at least 8 hours							
5. wash hair							
6. comb or brush hair							
7. exercise for 1 hour							
8. floss once							

Health

Name _____

Smart kids follow safety rules to remain healthy and safe. Draw the correct code symbol next to each rule.

car safety

water safety

walking safety

bike safety

poison safety

1. Get in and out on the curb side of a parked car.

2. Keep labels on all containers.

3. Wear white when riding in twilight.

4. Always walk on sidewalks, not in the street.

5. Ride in the same direction as the moving cars.

6. Be sure your bike is in good working order.

7. Tighten caps on containers after using.

8. Do not run on swimming pool decks.

9. Stay back at railroad crossings.

10. Look both ways before crossing a road.

11. Always wear a life preserver while boating.

12. Be sure your bike has lights and reflectors.

13. Keep the poison control number near your phone.

14. Always swim with a buddy.

15. While walking, follow traffic lights and signs.

16. Always keep car doors locked.

17. Swim only in approved marked areas with an adult present.

18. Cross streets only at corners.

IF8785 Third Grade in Review

Health

Name _____

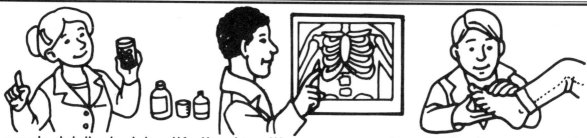

Read each riddle to identify the health career worker. Write the career in each box.

I check eyes and prescribe glasses when needed. _____	I warn of the dangers of drugs and alcohol. _____	I fit teeth for braces and other appliances. _____
I check to see that all body systems are working properly. _____	I supervise exercise programs. _____	I plan well-balanced meals for good nutrition. _____
I check feet for problems. _____	I help solve emotional problems. _____	I clean teeth and make needed repairs. _____
I keep athletes' bodies in good physical condition. _____	I repair bones when they are broken. _____	I fill prescriptions written by doctors for medicine. _____

Word Bank

orthodontist	doctor	podiatrist
psychologist	optometrist	drug counselor
dietician	pharmacist	sports medicine
dentist	orthopedist	fitness coach

Answer Key
Third Grade
in Review

English

Name _____

Write each set of words in the correct order to make a sentence. The first word is underlined.

1. floors our in <u>There</u> school are two
There are two floors in our school.

2. is mascot a school bulldog <u>Our</u>
Our school mascot is a bulldog.

3. kindergarten just sister started <u>My</u>
My sister just started Kindergarten.

4. <u>Math</u> is subject favorite my
Math is my favorite subject.

5. on street <u>What</u> is school your
What street is your school on?

6. minivan drives blue <u>My</u> a teacher
My teacher drives a blue minivan.

7. delicious cafeteria <u>Our</u> pizza serves
Our cafeteria serves delicious pizza.

8. your name is principal's <u>What</u>
What is your principal's name?

9. in <u>We</u> hockey gym played floor
We played floor hockey in gym.

10. May in show <u>Our</u> art school had an
Our school had an art show in May.

11. won spelling friend <u>My</u> contest best the
My best friend won the spelling contest.

12. <u>I</u> perfect award received an attendance for
I received an award for perfect attendance.

Page 1

English

Name _____

Number each set of words in alphabetical order.

4 blue	3 dark	2 green
1 blame	1 damp	4 grumpy
2 blister	4 day	3 grown
3 block	2 dandy	1 grapes

2 sheet	1 plaster	1 mob
4 shoe	3 plot	3 more
3 shiny	4 ply	2 money
1 shake	2 please	4 most

1 cream	1 wrap	3 problem
3 croak	2 wren	2 pretty
2 cricket	3 wrist	1 pray
4 cruel	4 wrong	4 prune

1 track	3 sticky	1 back
4 troll	1 stamp	4 battery
2 treat	4 stomp	3 bandit
3 trip	2 steam	2 bad

4 foul	4 clock	3 land
2 for	3 clip	2 lamp
1 fond	2 clear	4 last
3 foster	1 clank	1 ladder

Page 2

English

Name _____

Add the correct punctuation mark in the color shown on the crayon.

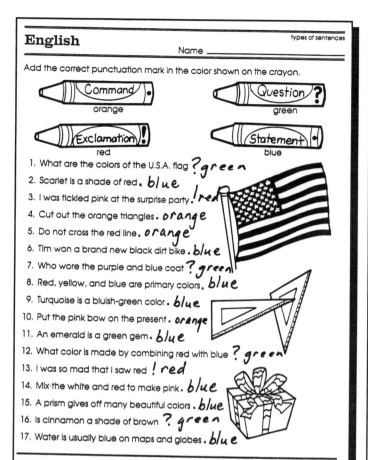

Command . — orange
Question ? — green
Exclamation ! — red
Statement . — blue

1. What are the colors of the U.S.A. flag ? *green*
2. Scarlet is a shade of red . *blue*
3. I was tickled pink at the surprise party ! *red*
4. Cut out the orange triangles . *orange*
5. Do not cross the red line . *orange*
6. Tim won a brand new black dirt bike . *blue*
7. Who wore the purple and blue coat ? *green*
8. Red, yellow, and blue are primary colors . *blue*
9. Turquoise is a bluish-green color . *blue*
10. Put the pink bow on the present . *orange*
11. An emerald is a green gem . *blue*
12. What color is made by combining red with blue ? *green*
13. I was so mad that I saw red ! *red*
14. Mix the white and red to make pink . *blue*
15. A prism gives off many beautiful colors . *blue*
16. Is cinnamon a shade of brown ? *green*
17. Water is usually blue on maps and globes . *blue*

Page 3

English

Name _____

Draw a pair of scissors between the subject and predicate of each sentence.

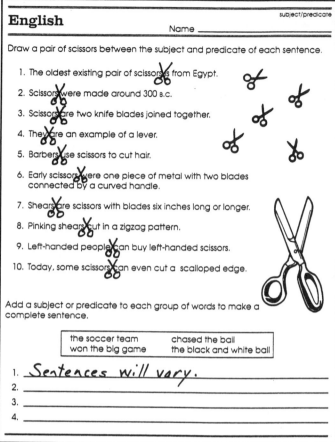

1. The oldest existing pair of scissors ✂ is from Egypt.
2. Scissors ✂ were made around 300 B.C.
3. Scissors ✂ are two knife blades joined together.
4. They ✂ are an example of a lever.
5. Barbers ✂ use scissors to cut hair.
6. Early scissors ✂ were one piece of metal with two blades connected by a curved handle.
7. Shears ✂ are scissors with blades six inches long or longer.
8. Pinking shears ✂ cut in a zigzag pattern.
9. Left-handed people ✂ can buy left-handed scissors.
10. Today, some scissors ✂ can even cut a scalloped edge.

Add a subject or predicate to each group of words to make a complete sentence.

| the soccer team | chased the ball |
| won the big game | the black and white ball |

1. _Sentences will vary._
2. _____
3. _____
4. _____

Page 4

English

Name _____

In the lower bunk bed, write a synonym for the word in the upper bunk bed. Then color the bed containing the word that would come first in ABC order.

Word Bank

couch	pretty	injured	miniature
intelligent	chilly	difficult	under
frightened	tardy	pier	light

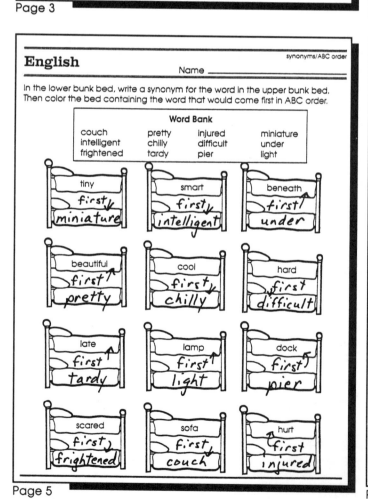

- tiny / *miniature*
- smart / *intelligent*
- beneath / *under*
- beautiful / *pretty*
- cool / *chilly*
- hard / *difficult*
- late / *tardy*
- lamp / *light*
- dock / *pier*
- scared / *frightened*
- sofa / *couch*
- hurt / *injured*

Page 5

English

Name _____

Find the matching antonym for each word listed under the anthills. Then draw the correct number of ants on each anthill to show the number of the matching antonym.

1. under	5. hot	9. lower	13. thin
2. south	6. awake	10. hard	14. rested
3. play	7. dirty	11. leave	15. last
4. empty	8. dull	12. melt	16. light

cold   full   thick   first

tired   dark   north   work

shiny   freeze   higher   clean

easy   asleep   over   arrive

Page 6

IF8785 Third Grade in Review

Page 7

Name _____

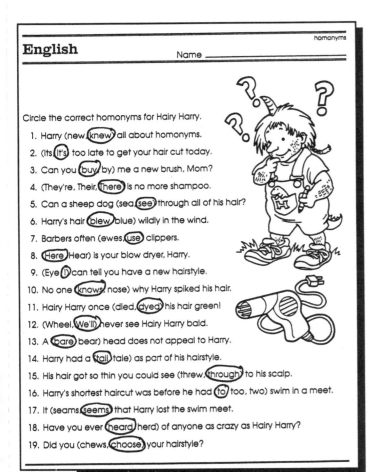

Circle the correct homonyms for Hairy Harry.

1. Harry (new, *knew*) all about homonyms.
2. (Its, *It's*) too late to get your hair cut today.
3. Can you (*buy*, by) me a new brush, Mom?
4. (They're, Their, *There*) is no more shampoo.
5. Can a sheep dog (sea, *see*) through all of his hair?
6. Harry's hair (*blew*, blue) wildly in the wind.
7. Barbers often (ewes, *use*) clippers.
8. (*Here*, Hear) is your blow dryer, Harry.
9. (Eye, *I*) can tell you have a new hairstyle.
10. No one (*knows*, nose) why Harry spiked his hair.
11. Hairy Harry once (died, *dyed*) his hair green!
12. (Wheel, *We'll*) never see Hairy Harry bald.
13. A (*bare*, bear) head does not appeal to Harry.
14. Harry had a (*tail*, tale) as part of his hairstyle.
15. His hair got so thin you could see (threw, *through*) to his scalp.
16. Harry's shortest haircut was before he had (*to*, too, two) swim in a meet.
17. It (seams, *seems*) that Harry lost the swim meet.
18. Have you ever (*heard*, herd) of anyone as crazy as Hairy Harry?
19. Did you (chews, *choose*) your hairstyle?

Page 7

Page 8

Name _____

Read the dictionary entry for *dugout*, then follow the directions below.

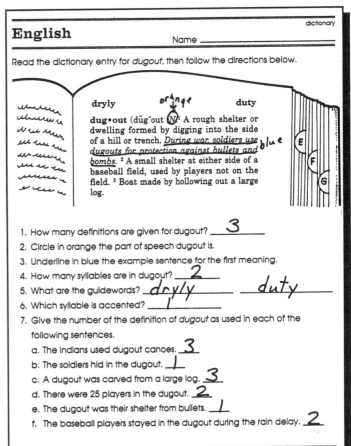

dryly   duty

dug•out (dŭg´out) *N.* 1 A rough shelter or dwelling formed by digging into the side of a hill or trench. *During war, soldiers use dugouts for protection against bullets and bombs.* 2 A small shelter at either side of a baseball field, used by players not on the field. 3 Boat made by hollowing out a large log.

1. How many definitions are given for dugout? __3__
2. Circle in orange the part of speech dugout is.
3. Underline in blue the example sentence for the first meaning.
4. How many syllables are in dugout? __2__
5. What are the guidewords? __dryly__ __duty__
6. Which syllable is accented?
7. Give the number of the definition of *dugout* as used in each of the following sentences.
   a. The Indians used dugout canoes. __3__
   b. The soldiers hid in the dugout. __1__
   c. A dugout was carved from a large log. __3__
   d. There were 25 players in the dugout. __2__
   e. The dugout was their shelter from bullets. __1__
   f. The baseball players stayed in the dugout during the rain delay. __2__

Page 8

Page 9

Name _____

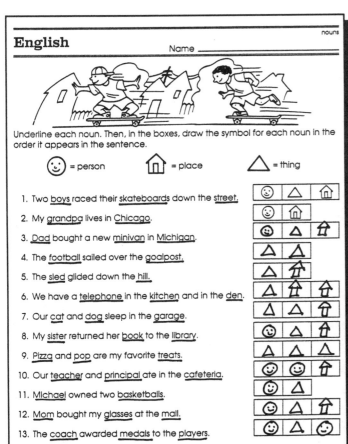

Underline each noun. Then, in the boxes, draw the symbol for each noun in the order it appears in the sentence.

☺ = person   ⌂ = place   △ = thing

1. Two boys raced their skateboards down the street.
2. My grandpa lives in Chicago.
3. Dad bought a new minivan in Michigan.
4. The football sailed over the goalpost.
5. The sled glided down the hill.
6. We have a telephone in the kitchen and in the den.
7. Our cat and dog sleep in the garage.
8. My sister returned her book to the library.
9. Pizza and pop are my favorite treats.
10. Our teacher and principal ate in the cafeteria.
11. Michael owned two basketballs.
12. Mom bought my glasses at the mall.
13. The coach awarded medals to the players.

Page 9

Page 10

Name _____

Draw a red around each singular noun, and a yellow around each plural noun. Then add green plants and blue waves to the fish tank.

red starfish
red tadpole
yellow eggs
red or yellow seaweed
yellow seas
red whale
yellow flakes
red snail
yellow turtles
yellow bubbles
yellow guppies
red minnow
red sea horse
yellow tanks
red lilypad
yellow seashells
yellow dolphins

Page 10

IF8785 Third Grade in Review

Page 11

English

Name _____

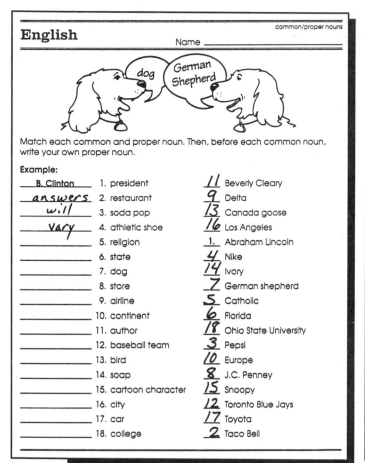

Match each common and proper noun. Then, before each common noun, write your own proper noun.

Example:

B. Clinton	1. president	_11_	Beverly Cleary
answers	2. restaurant	_9_	Delta
will	3. soda pop	_13_	Canada goose
vary	4. athletic shoe	_16_	Los Angeles
	5. religion	_1_	Abraham Lincoln
	6. state	_4_	Nike
	7. dog	_14_	Ivory
	8. store	_7_	German shepherd
	9. airline	_5_	Catholic
	10. continent	_6_	Florida
	11. author	_18_	Ohio State University
	12. baseball team	_3_	Pepsi
	13. bird	_10_	Europe
	14. soap	_8_	J.C. Penney
	15. cartoon character	_15_	Snoopy
	16. city	_12_	Toronto Blue Jays
	17. car	_17_	Toyota
	18. college	_2_	Taco Bell

Page 11

Page 12

English

Name _____

In each ⌣ write a pronoun that could take the place of the underlined noun(s).

Example: (He) Bob saw the movie twice.

(its) 1. The cat chased the cat's tail.

(They) 2. Grandma and Grandpa moved to Florida.

(She) 3. My sister was born in July.

(them) 4. We gave the puppy to our neighbors.

(We) 5. Rick and I played soccer on Monday.

(Her) 6. Ashley's mom will drive us to school.

(us) 7. Please give your coat to Kim and me.

(It) 8. The chair was missing one rung.

(his) 9. We played against Justin's team.

(We) 10. My family and I went to Disney World.

(him) 11. Take your homework to Mr. Strayer.

(They) 12. My cousins live in California.

(her) 13. We went to see Sue in the hospital.

(us) 14. Brent gave his lunch to Greg and me.

(We) 15. Megan and Barb played tennis.

(it) 16. Where was the car supposed to be parked?

Page 12

Page 13

English

Name _____

Write the abbreviation above each word.

Dr. / doctor	Jan. / January	St. / street
Mrs. / married woman	Ave. / avenue	lb. / pound
Rd. / road	Mt. / mountain	Mr. / mister
Apt. / apartment	in. / inch	Doz. / dozen
Ms. / woman	P.O. / post office	cm / centimeter
Qt. / quart	M.P.H. / miles per hour	Aug. / August
F / Fahrenheit	Dept. / department	Jr. / junior

Page 13

Page 14

English

Name _____

Write two verbs for each object.

Example:

Answers will vary.

fly
land

Now draw something that goes with each pair of verbs.

| hiss / slither | gallop / trot | fly / chirp | slam / lock |

Page 14

IF8785 Third Grade in Review

Page 15

English

Name _____

Write a letter to the President of the United States. Then draw a colored box around each part of a friendly letter as directed below.

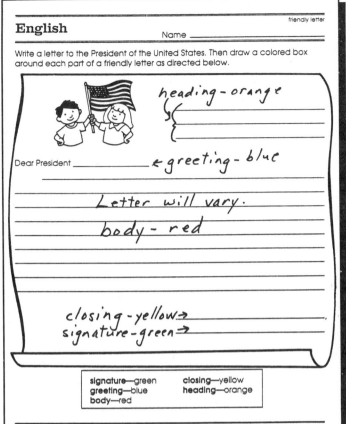

heading - orange

Dear President _____ ← greeting - blue

_____

Letter will vary.

body - red

closing - yellow →
signature - green →

signature—green	closing—yellow
greeting—blue	heading—orange
body—red	

Page 16

English

Name _____

Write two adjectives in each pair of glasses to describe each noun.

Answers will vary.

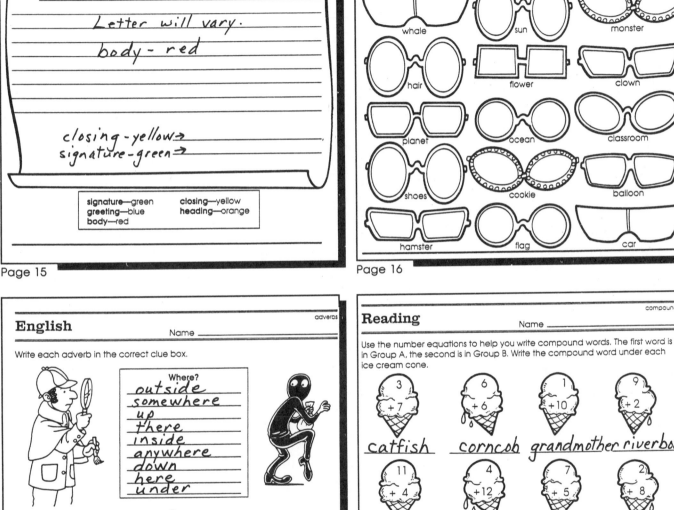

eyes mice sandwich

clouds voice turkey

whale sun monster

hair flower clown

planet ocean classroom

shoes cookie balloon

hamster flag car

Page 17

English

Name _____

Write each adverb in the correct clue box.

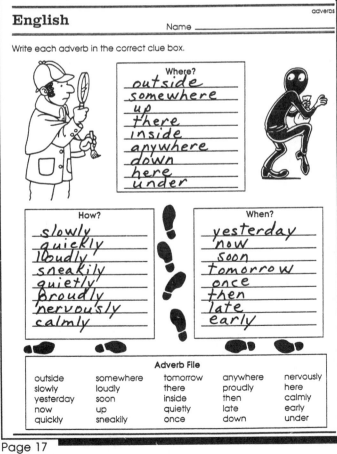

Where?
outside
somewhere
up
there
inside
anywhere
down
here
under

How?
slowly
quickly
loudly
sneakily
quietly
proudly
nervously
calmly

When?
yesterday
now
soon
tomorrow
once
then
late
early

Adverb File

outside	somewhere	tomorrow	anywhere	nervously
slowly	loudly	there	proudly	here
yesterday	soon	inside	then	calmly
now	up	quietly	late	early
quickly	sneakily	once	down	under

Page 18

Reading

Name _____

Use the number equations to help you write compound words. The first word is in Group A, the second is in Group B. Write the compound word under each ice cream cone.

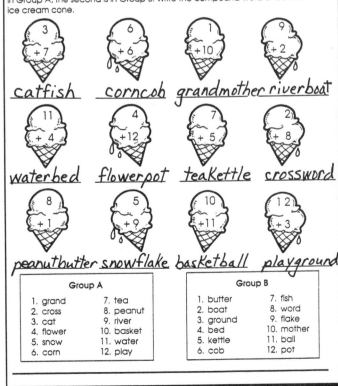

$3 + 7$ catfish $6 + 6$ corncob $1 + 10$ grandmother $9 + 2$ riverboat

$11 + 4$ waterbed $4 + 12$ flowerpot $7 + 5$ teakettle $2 + 8$ crossword

$8 + 1$ peanutbutter $5 + 9$ snowflake $10 + 11$ basketball $12 + 3$ playground

Group A		Group B	
1. grand	7. tea	1. butter	7. fish
2. cross	8. peanut	2. boat	8. word
3. cat	9. river	3. ground	9. flake
4. flower	10. basket	4. bed	10. mother
5. snow	11. water	5. kettle	11. ball
6. corn	12. play	6. cob	12. pot

Reading

Name _____

Get on the right track with contractions. Write the contraction for each pair of words in the matching car of the train.

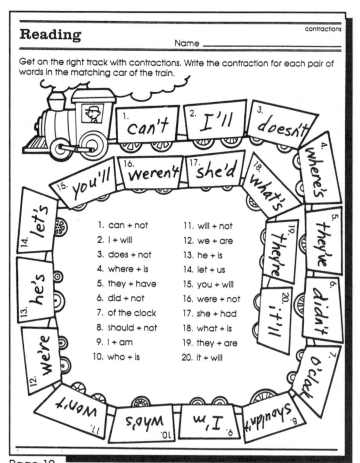

1. can + not
2. I + will
3. does + not
4. where + is
5. they + have
6. did + not
7. of the clock
8. should + not
9. I + am
10. who + is
11. will + not
12. we + are
13. he + is
14. let + us
15. you + will
16. were + not
17. she + had
18. what + is
19. they + are
20. it + will

Page 19

Reading

Name _____

Write a prefix for each base word. Then write the points scored by using that prefix. Tally your final score on the scoreboard.

Final Score

dis/re connect	**pre/re** view	**dis/un/re** cover	**pre** fix
___ points	___ points	___ points	___ points
im polite	**un** caring	**re** call	**un/re** finished
___ points	___ points	___ points	___ points
un/re make	**dis/pre** tend	**un** believable	**re/un** bound
___ points	___ points	___ points	___ points
re start	**pre/re** heat	**dis/re** charge	**un** kind
___ points	___ points	___ points	___ points
im possible	**un/re** tied	**un/re** locked	**im/re** port
___ points	___ points	___ points	___ points

Scoreboard: pre = 2, dis = 4, im = 5, un = 1, re = 3

Page 20

Reading

Name _____

Write a suffix for each base word. Color the snakes as shown.

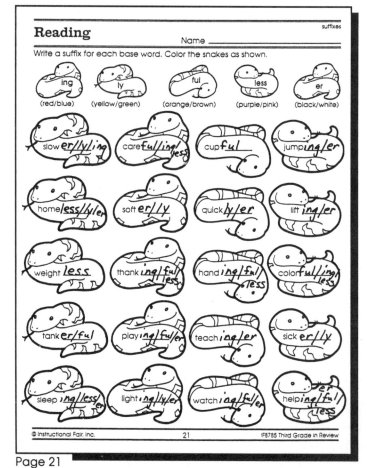

ing (red/blue)   ly (yellow/green)   ful (orange/brown)   less (purple/pink)   er (black/white)

slow **er/ly/ing**   care **ful/ing/less**   cup **ful**   jump **ing/er**

home **less/ly/er**   soft **er/ly**   quick **ly/er**   lift **ing/er**

weight **less**   thank **ing/ful/less**   hand **ing/ful/less**   color **ful/ing/less**

tank **er/ful**   play **ing/ful**   teach **ing/er**   sick **er/ly**

sleep **ing/less**   light **ing/ly/er**   watch **ing/ful/er**   help **ing/ful/less**

© Instructional Fair, Inc.   21   IF8785 Third Grade in Review

Page 21

Reading

Name _____

Count the syllables in each word. Draw that number of gumballs in each machine.

gumballs   rapidly   important   unsuccessful

video   picnic   fantastic   machine

disappearing   bubble   camera   treat

beautiful   motorcycle   lightning   gasoline

encyclopedia   syllable   community   camper

pillow   dictionary   orange   title

Page 22

Name _____

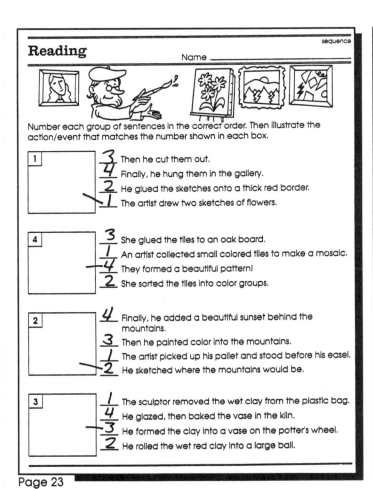

Number each group of sentences in the correct order. Then illustrate the action/event that matches the number shown in each box.

1
- 3 Then he cut them out.
- 4 Finally, he hung them in the gallery.
- 2 He glued the sketches onto a thick red border.
- 1 The artist drew two sketches of flowers.

4
- 3 She glued the tiles to an oak board.
- 1 An artist collected small colored tiles to make a mosaic.
- 4 They formed a beautiful pattern!
- 2 She sorted the tiles into color groups.

2
- 4 Finally, he added a beautiful sunset behind the mountains.
- 3 Then he painted color into the mountains.
- 1 The artist picked up his pallet and stood before his easel.
- 2 He sketched where the mountains would be.

3
- 1 The sculptor removed the wet clay from the plastic bag.
- 4 He glazed, then baked the vase in the kiln.
- 3 He formed the clay into a vase on the potter's wheel.
- 2 He rolled the wet red clay into a large ball.

Page 23

Name _____

Write the long vowel for each word. Draw the object inside each pyramid.

Example:

a ngel

h **o** se   **i** ce cream   b **o** ne

ch **e** ese   cr **a** yon   sh **e** ep

k **i** te   t **o** ast   b **o** wl

Page 24

Name _____

ă   ĕ   ĭ   ŏ   ŭ

Write the missing vowel for each word. Then draw the correct short vowel pattern on each teepee.

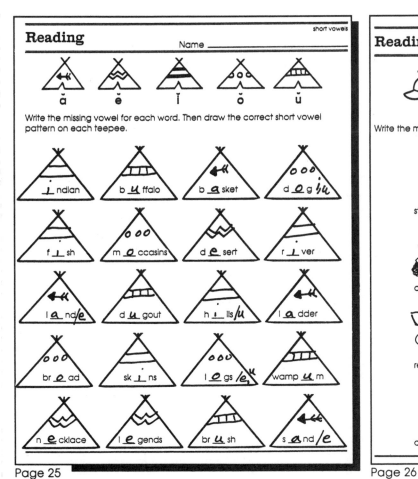

i ndian   b **u** ffalo   b **a** sket   d **o** g

f **i** sh   m **o** ccasins   d **e** sert   r **i** ver

l **a** nd/e   d **u** gout   h **i** lls   l **a** dder

br **e** ad   sk **i** ns   l **o** gs/e   wamp **u** m

n **e** cklace   l **e** gends   br **u** sh   s **a** nd/e

Page 25

Name _____

oa   ou   ai   ea   ie

Write the missing vowel pair on each line. Draw the correct hat on each face.

st **ea** m   r **ou** nd   t **oa** d

afr **ai** d   p **ie** crust   w **ai** st

rel **ie** f   gr **ou** nd hog   ch **ie** f

ah **ea** d   t **oa** ster   qu **ai** l

Page 26

Add the correct **r-controlled vowel**. Then write the words in the correct house.

c a r penter   c a r pet   refrigerat o r
b i r thplace   r u r al   b i r dbath
f u r niture   s u r vey   wallpap e r
st o r m   st o r eroom   f i r eplace
flow e r s   libr a r y   carp o r t
g a r age   c u r tains   dishwash e r

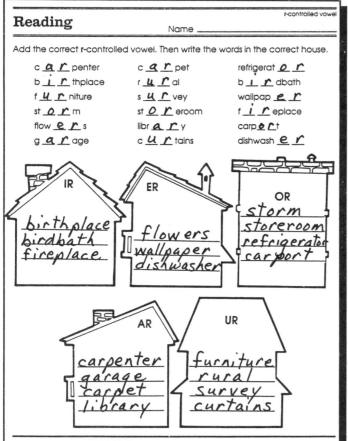

IR
birthplace
birdbath
fireplace

ER
flowers
wallpaper
dishwasher

OR
storm
storeroom
refrigerator
carport

AR
carpenter
garage
carpet
library

UR
furniture
rural
survey
curtains

Write the missing blend in each word. Then color the bow the correct color.

bl	tr	pr	st	fl	cl	dr
(red)	(green)	(blue)	(yellow)	(orange)	(pink)	(purple)

blue — pr esent
purple — dr ess pr bl
orange — fl owers bl
bl st pink fi cl ock

pink — cl amps st tr
green — tr easure
purple — dr ums
red — bl ouse

blue — pr izes
orange — fl ippers cl
pink — cl othes
pink — cl own bl, fl

yellow — st opwatch
red — bl ender
green — tr actor
blue — pr incess

orange — fl ashlight
yellow — st ickers tr, pr, fl
bl anket
st ove pr, cl, dr

Write the missing consonant blend.

ph	ck	sh	rt	ct
st	nt	nd	ld	ch

Example:

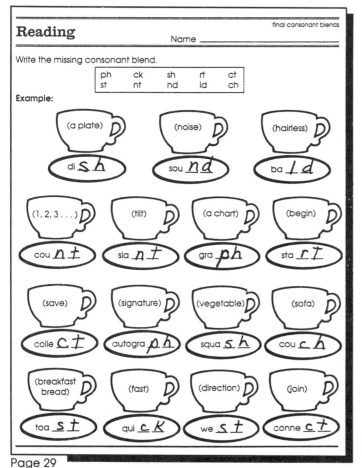

(a plate) di s h
(noise) sou n d
(hairless) ba l d

(1, 2, 3 . . .) cou n t
(tilt) sla n t
(a chart) gra ph
(begin) sta r t

(save) colle c t
(signature) autogra ph
(vegetable) squa s h
(sofa) cou c h

(breakfast bread) toa s t
(fast) qui c k
(direction) we s t
(join) conne c t

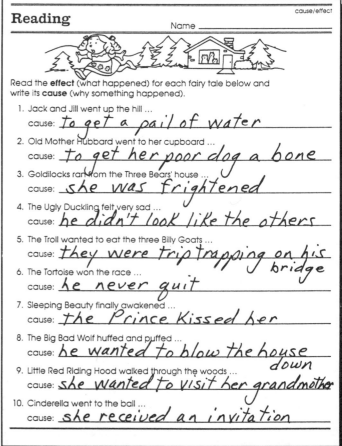

Read the **effect** (what happened) for each fairy tale below and write its **cause** (why something happened).

1. Jack and Jill went up the hill ...
   cause: To get a pail of water

2. Old Mother Hubbard went to her cupboard ...
   cause: To get her poor dog a bone

3. Goldilocks ran from the Three Bears' house ...
   cause: she was frightened

4. The Ugly Duckling felt very sad ...
   cause: he didn't look like the others

5. The Troll wanted to eat the three Billy Goats ...
   cause: they were trip trapping on his bridge

6. The Tortoise won the race ...
   cause: he never quit

7. Sleeping Beauty finally awakened ...
   cause: the Prince kissed her

8. The Big Bad Wolf huffed and puffed ...
   cause: he wanted to blow the house down

9. Little Red Riding Hood walked through the woods ...
   cause: she wanted to visit her grandmother

10. Cinderella went to the ball ...
    cause: she received an invitation

---

fact/opinion

Name _____

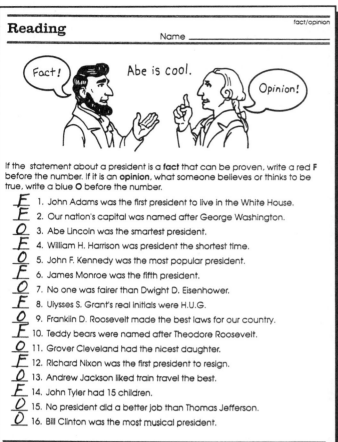

Fact! Abe is cool. **Opinion!**

If the statement about a president is a **fact** that can be proven, write a red **F** before the number. If it is an **opinion**, what someone believes or thinks to be true, write a blue **O** before the number.

F 1. John Adams was the first president to live in the White House.
F 2. Our nation's capital was named after George Washington.
O 3. Abe Lincoln was the smartest president.
F 4. William H. Harrison was president the shortest time.
O 5. John F. Kennedy was the most popular president.
F 6. James Monroe was the fifth president.
O 7. No one was fairer than Dwight D. Eisenhower.
F 8. Ulysses S. Grant's real initials were H.U.G.
O 9. Franklin D. Roosevelt made the best laws for our country.
F 10. Teddy bears were named after Theodore Roosevelt.
O 11. Grover Cleveland had the nicest daughter.
F 12. Richard Nixon was the first president to resign.
O 13. Andrew Jackson liked train travel the best.
F 14. John Tyler had 15 children.
O 15. No president did a better job than Thomas Jefferson.
O 16. Bill Clinton was the most musical president.

Page 31

---

double consonants

Name _____

Write the missing double consonants.

le **tt** er   a **cc** ount   ru **nn** er

gl **gg** le   ca **ll** ing   bu **bb** le

hi **ss** ing   wa **ff** le   ha **mm** er

no **zz** le   go **bb** le   babysi **tt** er

wi **gg** le   sto **pp** ing   pu **dd** le

gue **ss** ing   ki **tt** en   ra **cc** oon

hi **pp** opotamus   a **pp** le   o **tt** er

sto **pp** er   spa **rr** ow   ga **ll** on

Page 32

---

following directions

Name _____

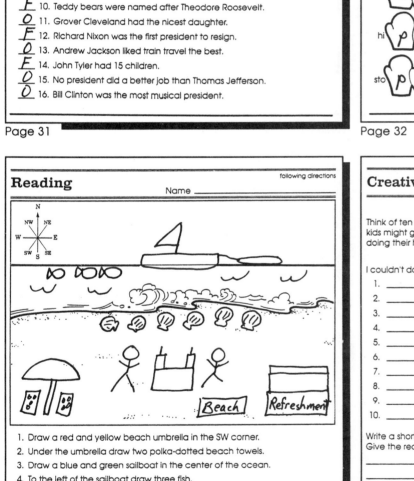

Beach   Refreshment

1. Draw a red and yellow beach umbrella in the SW corner.
2. Under the umbrella draw two polka-dotted beach towels.
3. Draw a blue and green sailboat in the center of the ocean.
4. To the left of the sailboat draw three fish.
5. Draw a refreshment stand in the SE corner of the beach.
6. Draw six seashells along the coastline.
7. Draw a purple and pink surfboard tied to the sailboat.
8. Make a sandcastle in the center of the beach area.
9. Draw two children, one on each side of the sandcastle.
10. Color several blue and green wave lines (‿) in the water.
11. Make up a name for the beach. Draw a sign with the beach's name left of the refreshment stand.

Page 33

---

reasoning

Name _____

Think of ten funny, creative reasons kids might give their teacher for not doing their homework.

I couldn't do my homework because ...
1. Answers will vary.
2. _____
3. _____
4. _____
5. _____
6. _____
7. _____
8. _____
9. _____
10. _____

Write a short story telling about a time you didn't complete your homework. Give the reason why and explain what happened because it wasn't completed.

Story will vary.
_____
_____
_____
_____
_____
_____

Page 34

Creative Writing

Name _____

Become a composer. Write your own silly songs using these familiar melodies.

I. (Yankee Doodle) ☆ ☆ ☆ *Answers will vary.*

_____ _____ came to _____

Upon a _____ _____ .

He stuck a _____ in his_____

And called it _____ .

_____ _____ keep it up, _____

_____ _____

Mind the music and the _____

And with the _____ be _____ .

II. (Three Blind Mice)

Three _____ _____ , Three _____ _____ ,

See how they _____ , See how they _____ ,

They all ran after the _____ 's _____

Who cut off their tails with a _____ _____ ,

Did you ever see such a _____ in your life,

As three _____ _____

III. (If You're Happy and You Know It)

If you're happy and you know it, _____ _____ _____

If you're happy and you know it, _____ _____ _____

If you're happy and you know it,

Then your _____ will surely _____ _____

If you're happy and you know it, _____ _____ _____ ,

Page 35

Creative Writing

Name _____

This letter fell into the wrong paws! Snoopy tore and ate part of Charlie Brown's letter to Lucy. Finish the letter for Charlie.

Answers will vary.

Dear Lucy,
     I've often wondered why you are so _____ .
Every fall, you grab the _____
out from under me when I am trying to _____ .
No wonder I call you names like _____
and Crabby.
     Then, when I need _____
I come to your booth and you charge me _____
but I never _____
It makes me _____
Can't you please change how you _____ .

                    Your friend,
                    Charlie Brown

P.S. My head is not shaped like a _____

Page 36

Creative Writing

Name _____

Create your own cartoons for these comic strips. Use speech bubbles.

Cartoons will vary.

GARFIELD			
PEANUTS			
DENNIS THE MENACE			
ZIGGY			

Create a cartoon starring your own pet.

Page 37

Creative Writing

Name _____

For your birthday this year, you were allowed to take three friends on a hot-air balloon adventure for one day. Write about who you took and where you went. Use details to answer who, what, when, where, and why.

Stories will vary.

_____
_____
_____
_____
_____
_____
_____
_____
_____
_____
_____
_____
_____
_____
_____

Page 38

Creative Writing

Name _____

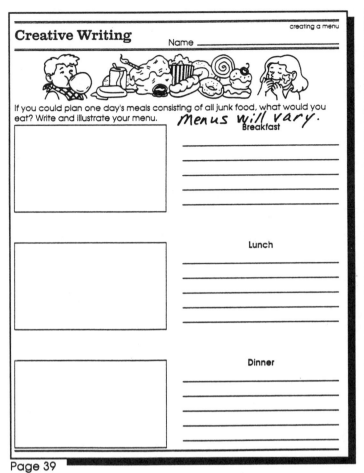

If you could plan one day's meals consisting of all junk food, what would you eat? Write and illustrate your menu.

Menus will vary.

Breakfast

_____
_____
_____
_____

Lunch

_____
_____
_____
_____

Dinner

_____
_____
_____
_____

Page 39

Critical Thinking

Name _____

Let's see how much you know. Answer each question very carefully.

1. Who does the Washington Monument honor? **Washington**
2. How many cookies are in an empty cookie jar? **0**
3. How many minutes are in a 3-minute hourglass? **3**
4. A pair of shoes is how many shoes? **2**
5. Where was the Vietnam War fought? **Vietnam**
6. The Ohio River was named for which state? **Ohio**
7. How do you spell hippopotamus? **hippopotamus**
8. What was President John F. Kennedy's last name? **Kennedy**
9. All aboard Flight 746 died in the crash. How many survivors were there? **0**
10. What is the product of 9 x 8 x 7 x 6 x 5 x 4 x 3 x 2 x 1 x 0? **0**
11. Lay a penny, nickel, and dime on the table to help you work this problem. Jordan's mom had three kids. She named the first one Penny, the second one Nickel. What did she name the third child? **Jordan**
12. How many pigs were in the tale, *The Three Little Pigs*? **3**
13. Who wrote the autobiography of Abraham Lincoln? **Lincoln**
14. How many months have 28 days? **all 12**

Page 40

Math

Name _____

Choose a partner. Each of you will need a copy of the grid. You can share a pair of dice. One player rolls the dice. Add the numbers and enter the answer in the correct square on the grid. If that square is full, you lose your turn. The first player to fill the grid wins.

Example: 🎲 + 🎲 = 9   (Enter in either the square for 3 + 6 or 6 + 3)

+	6	2	5	4	1	3
5	11	7	10	9	6	8
1	7	3	6	5	2	4
3	9	5	8	7	4	6
6	12	8	11	10	7	9
2	8	4	7	6	3	5
4	10	6	9	8	5	7

Page 41

Math

Name _____

Use the code on the satellite panels to answer the problems.

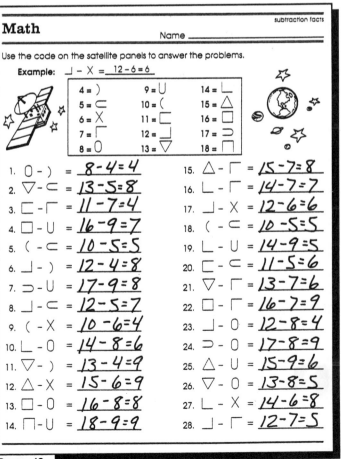

Example: ⌐ − ✕ = $12 - 6 = 6$

4 =)		9 = ∪	14 = ∟
5 = ⊏		10 = (	15 = △
6 = ✕		11 = ⊏	16 = ▢
7 = ⌐		12 = ⌐	17 = ⊃
8 = ○		13 = ▽	18 = ⊓

1. ○ −) = $8 - 4 = 4$
2. ▽ − ⊏ = $13 - 5 = 8$
3. ⊏ − ⌐ = $11 - 7 = 4$
4. ▢ − ∪ = $16 - 9 = 7$
5. (− ⊏ = $10 - 5 = 5$
6. ⌐ −) = $12 - 4 = 8$
7. ⊃ − ∪ = $17 - 9 = 8$
8. ⌐ − ⊏ = $12 - 5 = 7$
9. (− ✕ = $10 - 6 = 4$
10. ∟ − ○ = $14 - 8 = 6$
11. ▽ −) = $13 - 4 = 9$
12. △ − ✕ = $15 - 6 = 9$
13. ▢ − ○ = $16 - 8 = 8$
14. ⊓ − ∪ = $18 - 9 = 9$
15. △ − ⌐ = $15 - 7 = 8$
16. ∟ − ⌐ = $14 - 7 = 7$
17. ⌐ − ✕ = $12 - 6 = 6$
18. (− ⊏ = $10 - 5 = 5$
19. ∟ − ∪ = $14 - 9 = 5$
20. ⊏ − ⊏ = $11 - 5 = 6$
21. ▽ − ⌐ = $13 - 7 = 6$
22. ▢ − ⌐ = $16 - 7 = 9$
23. ⌐ − ○ = $12 - 8 = 4$
24. ⊃ − ○ = $17 - 8 = 9$
25. △ − ∪ = $15 - 9 = 6$
26. ▽ − ○ = $13 - 8 = 5$
27. ∟ − ✕ = $14 - 6 = 8$
28. ⌐ − ⌐ = $12 - 7 = 5$

Page 42

Page 43

Math

Name _____

Mathosaurus?

Work each problem.

6	7	5	9	3	8	7
9	4	7	6	8	4	5
+5	+8	+4	+7	+5	+8	+9
20	19	16	22	16	20	21

26	44	27	95	82	55	91
14	17	19	66	27	16	74
+35	+36	+43	+37	+67	+48	+55
75	97	89	198	176	119	220

306	418	821	752	616	519	803
217	562	159	307	148	425	555
+472	+334	+396	+921	+272	+395	+196
995	1314	1376	1980	1036	1339	1554

4011	5287	6179	7436	4343
2667	1694	3447	1814	2520
+1884	+3488	+2112	+2067	+8868
8562	10469	11738	11317	15731

8264	9041	7234	5214	1434
1137	5762	1695	1679	8082
+9038	+7730	+2524	+7740	+9848
18439	22533	11453	14633	19364

Page 43

Page 44

Math

Name _____

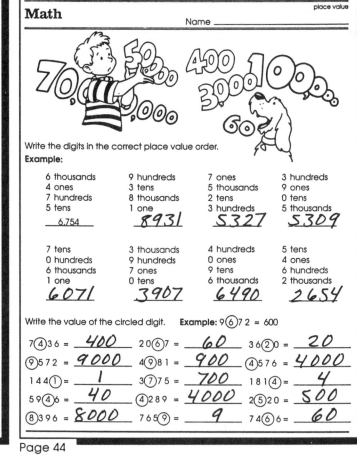

Write the digits in the correct place value order.

Example:

6 thousands	9 hundreds	7 ones	3 hundreds
4 ones	3 tens	5 thousands	9 ones
7 hundreds	8 thousands	2 tens	0 tens
5 tens	1 one	3 hundreds	5 thousands
6,754	8931	5327	5309

7 tens	3 thousands	4 hundreds	5 tens
0 hundreds	9 hundreds	0 ones	4 ones
6 thousands	7 ones	9 tens	6 hundreds
1 one	0 tens	6 thousands	2 thousands
6071	3907	6490	2654

Write the value of the circled digit.   **Example:** 9⑥72 = 600

7④36 = __400__   20⑥7 = __60__   36②0 = __20__

⑨572 = __9000__   4⑨81 = __900__   ④576 = __4000__

144① = __1__   3⑦75 = __700__   181④ = __4__

59④6 = __40__   ④289 = __4000__   2⑤20 = __500__

⑧396 = __8000__   765⑨ = __9__   74⑥6 = __60__

Page 44

Page 45

Math

Name _____

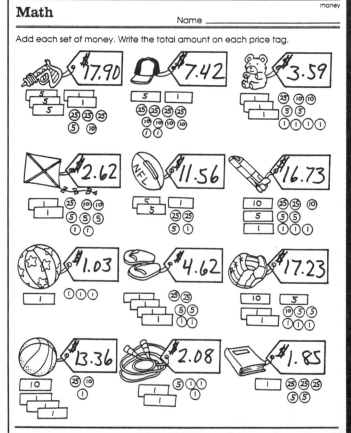

Work each problem on your calculator. Then, turn the calculator upside down and write the word which should match each clue.

	Answer	Clue	Word
Example: 256 + 362 =	618	antonym of small	Big
1. 139 + 524 =	663	a nest occupant	egg
2. 11,862 – 4,757 =	7105	a synonym for dirt	soil
3. 29,331 + 5,675 =	35006	a gander's husband	goose
4. 609 x 5 =	3045	a foot warmer	shoe
5. 12,955 – 9,251 =	3704	a gopher's home	hole
6. 323 x 25 =	8075	a messy, unkempt person	slob
7. 9,867 + 25,140 =	35007	an antonym of tight	loose
8. 2,428 ÷ 4 =	607	fireplace fuel	log
9. 10,436 – 3,102 =	7334	a foot's back section	heel
10. 918 x 6 =	5508	an employer	boss
11. 3,412 + 4,304 =	7716	a fish uses this to breathe	gill
12. 24,549 ÷ 7 =	3507	an antonym of win	lose
13. 8 x 50 + 9 x 2 =	818	keeps a baby clean	bib
14. 15 ÷ 3 x 103 =	515	another name for sister	sis
15. 5 x 60 + 4 =	304	gardening tool	hoe

Page 45

Page 46

Math

Name _____

Add each set of money. Write the total amount on each price tag.

$7.90 $7.42 $3.59

$2.62 $11.56 $16.73

$1.03 $4.62 $17.23

$13.36 $2.08 $1.85

Page 46

Page 47

Math

Name _____

time

Draw the hands on the clock to show the time given.

10:15	7:27	2:04	5:47
11:58	1:11	9:36	3:22
12:13	8:09	4:41	6:18
2:49	10:03	11:31	7:46

Page 47

Page 48

Math

Name _____

time

Read each sentence. Write the number of the matching clock by each sentence.

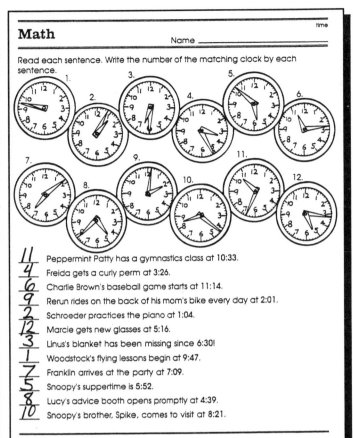

11 Peppermint Patty has a gymnastics class at 10:33.
4   Freida gets a curly perm at 3:26.
6   Charlie Brown's baseball game starts at 11:14.
9   Rerun rides on the back of his mom's bike every day at 2:01.
2   Schroeder practices the piano at 1:04.
12 Marcie gets new glasses at 5:16.
3   Linus's blanket has been missing since 6:30!
1   Woodstock's flying lessons begin at 9:47.
7   Franklin arrives at the party at 7:09.
5   Snoopy's suppertime is 5:52.
8   Lucy's advice booth opens promptly at 4:39.
10 Snoopy's brother, Spike, comes to visit at 8:21.

Page 48

Page 49

Math

Name _____

< > =

Work each problem. Then, compare the answers and write the correct sign (< > =) in the box.

Example:

| 6 − 4 [<] 3 + 5 | 12 − 6 [<] 6 + 8 | 9 + 4 [>] 8 + 3 |
| 2 . . . . 8 | 6 . . . . 14 | 13 . . . . 11 |

| 15 − 7 [=] 4 + 4 | 7 + 3 [>] 11 − 6 | 3 + 9 [<] 6 + 9 |
| 8 . . . . 8 | 10 . . . . 5 | 12 . . . . 15 |

| 18 − 9 [=] 4 + 5 | 7 + 7 [>] 13 − 5 | 14 − 8 [<] 11 − 4 |
| 9 . . . . 9 | 14 . . . . 8 | 6 . . . . 7 |

| 17 − 8 [<] 9 + 9 | 6 + 7 [=] 9 + 4 | 12 − 3 [>] 10 − 4 |
| 9 . . . . 18 | 13 . . . . 13 | 9 . . . . 6 |

| 5 + 7 [>] 8 + 2 | 15 − 6 [<] 3 + 7 | 16 − 7 [=] 8 + 1 |
| 12 . . . . 10 | 9 . . . . 10 | 9 . . . . 9 |

| 10 − 1 [>] 12 − 4 | 6 + 5 [<] 8 + 4 | 13 − 4 [>] 5 + 3 |
| 9 . . . . 8 | 11 . . . . 12 | 9 . . . . 8 |

| 7 + 3 [>] 11 − 2 | 8 − 4 [<] 14 − 9 | 3 + 8 [<] 8 + 6 |
| 10 . . . . 9 | 4 . . . . 5 | 11 . . . . 14 |

Page 49

Page 50

Math

Name _____

addition with regrouping

Work each problem. Then answer the riddle by writing the letter by each problem in the matching numbered blanks below.

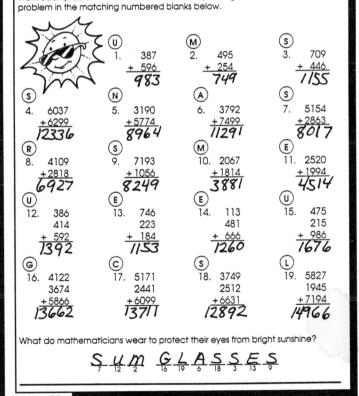

(U) 1.   387
      + 596
       983

(M) 2.   495
      + 254
       749

(S) 3.   709
      + 446
      1155

(S) 4.   6037
      + 6299
      12336

(N) 5.   3190
      + 5774
       8964

(A) 6.   3792
      + 7499
      11291

(S) 7.   5154
      + 2863
       8017

(R) 8.   4109
      + 2818
       6927

(S) 9.   7193
      + 1056
       8249

(M) 10. 2067
      + 1814
       3881

(E) 11. 2520
      + 1994
       4514

(U) 12.   386
          414
      + 592
       1392

(E) 13.   746
          223
      + 184
       1153

(E) 14.   113
          481
      + 666
       1260

(U) 15.   475
          215
      + 986
       1676

(G) 16. 4122
         3674
      + 5866
      13662

(C) 17. 5171
         2441
      + 6099
      13711

(S) 18. 3749
         2512
      + 6631
      12892

(L) 19. 5827
         1945
      + 7194
      14966

What do mathematicians wear to protect their eyes from bright sunshine?

S U M   G L A S S E S
7 12 2   16 19 6 18 3 13 9

Page 50

Page 51

Work each problem. Then write the letter by each problem in the matching numbered blanks below to complete the sentence.

(U) 1. 317 −198 = 119
(E) 2. 406 −257 = 149
(A) 3. 700 −351 = 349
(E) 4. 824 −517 = 307
(D) 5. 103 −77 = 26
(S) 6. 115 −69 = 46

(H) 7. 901 −452 = 449
(N) 8. 625 −133 = 492
(O) 9. 241 −37 = 204
(E) 10. 733 −546 = 187
(W) 11. 628 −544 = 84
(L) 12. 420 −175 = 245

(Y) 13. 882 −399 = 483
(S) 14. 450 −263 = 187
(T) 15. 505 −236 = 269
(I) 16. 147 −89 = 58
(S) 17. 902 −746 = 156
(U) 18. 646 −177 = 469

(S) 19. 303 −196 = 107
(I) 20. 132 −44 = 88
(T) 21. 618 −419 = 199
(V) 22. 700 −136 = 564
(A) 23. 201 −122 = 79
(T) 24. 934 −555 = 379

(T) 25. 821 −462 = 359
(G) 26. 838 −278 = 560
(O) 27. 951 −374 = 577
(Y) 28. 410 −369 = 41
(R) 29. 783 −255 = 528
(H) 30. 411 −262 = 149

Subtraction . . .
GIVES YOU LESS THAN YOU STARTED WITH!

Page 51

Page 52

Work the problems. Remember to put the "$" and "." in each answer. Circle any answer with a "1" in it. Then find the total of all answers with "1"s.

$7.46 + 8.25 = $15.71
$13.40 − 9.32 = $4.08
$3.58 + 9.94 = $13.52
$16.00 − 7.69 = $8.31
$4.04 + 2.27 = $6.31

$2.14 + 8.65 = $10.79
$26.19 − 15.43 = $10.76
$7.53 + 9.64 = $17.17
$10.01 − 7.17 = $2.84
$12.48 + 36.92 = $49.40

$5.75 + 1.63 = $7.38
$12.57 − 9.86 = $2.71
$9.87 + 4.15 = $14.02
$20.67 − 14.81 = $5.86
$6.62 + 4.39 = $11.01

$2.74 + 9.99 = $12.73
$11.32 − 5.66 = $5.66
$4.93 + 7.58 = $12.51
$15.00 − 3.34 = $11.66
$8.48 + 6.93 = $15.41

$5.25 + 1.79 = $7.04
$17.01 − 8.47 = $8.54
$6.89 + 7.73 = $14.62
$14.02 − 7.11 = $6.91
$5.38 + 8.74 = $14.12

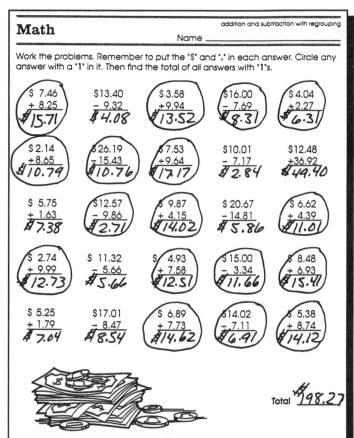

Total $198.27

Page 52

Page 53

Wiggle your way from the head of each snake to its tail, by adding and subtracting to reach the final answer.

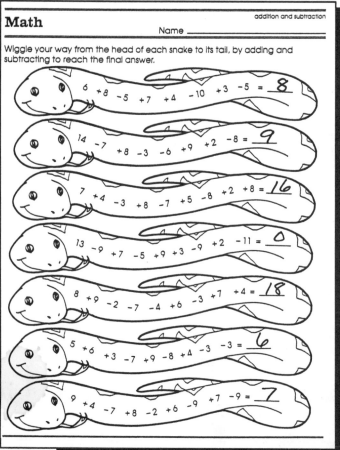

6 +8 −5 +7 +4 −10 +3 −5 = 8
14 −7 +8 −3 −6 +9 +2 −8 = 9
7 +4 −3 +8 −7 +5 −8 +2 +8 = 16
13 −9 +7 −5 +9 −3 −9 +2 −11 = 0
8 +9 −2 −7 −4 +6 −3 +7 +4 = 18
5 +6 +3 −7 +9 −8 +4 −3 −3 = 6
9 +4 −7 +8 −2 +6 −9 +7 −9 = 7

Page 53

Page 54

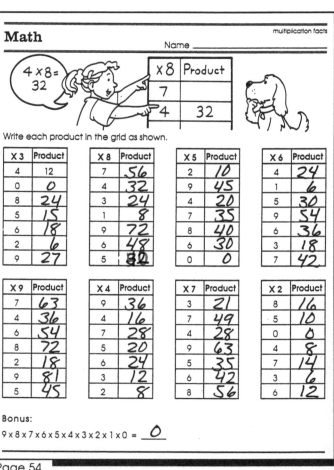

4 × 8 = 32

X8	Product
7	
4	32

Write each product in the grid as shown.

X 3	Product
4	12
0	0
8	24
5	15
6	18
2	6
9	27

X 8	Product
7	56
4	32
3	24
1	8
9	72
6	48
5	40

X 5	Product
2	10
9	45
4	20
7	35
8	40
6	30
0	0

X 6	Product
4	24
1	6
5	30
9	54
6	36
3	18
7	42

X 9	Product
7	63
4	36
6	54
8	72
2	18
9	81
5	45

X 4	Product
9	36
4	16
7	28
5	20
6	24
3	12
2	8

X 7	Product
3	21
7	49
4	28
9	63
5	35
6	42
8	56

X 2	Product
8	16
5	10
0	0
4	8
7	14
3	6
6	12

Bonus:

9 x 8 x 7 x 6 x 5 x 4 x 3 x 2 x 1 x 0 = 0

Page 54

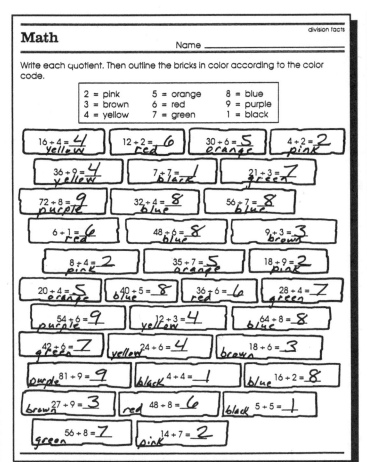

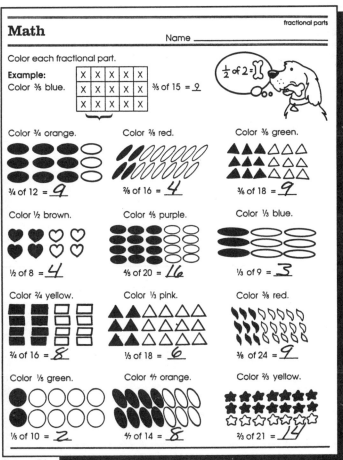

Page 59

Create each object using the geometric shapes indicated.

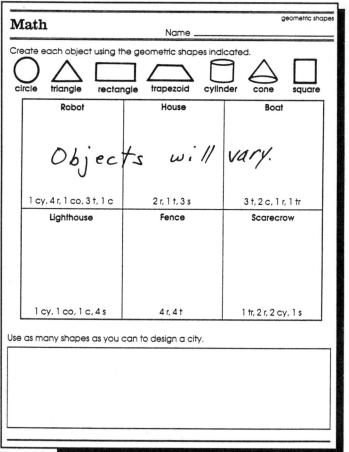

circle   triangle   rectangle   trapezoid   cylinder   cone   square

Robot	House	Boat
Objects will vary.		
1 cy, 4 r, 1 co, 3 t, 1 c	2 r, 1 t, 3 s	3 t, 2 c, 1 r, 1 tr
Lighthouse	**Fence**	**Scarecrow**
1 cy, 1 co, 1 c, 4 s	4 r, 4 t	1 tr, 2 r, 2 cy, 1 s

Use as many shapes as you can to design a city.

Page 60

Perimeter   Area

P = 2+2+1+1+1+3 = 10   A = 5

Perimeter is the distance around an area. **Area** is the space inside a shape. Find the perimeter and area for each shape using each square unit.

Example:

P = 20 units
A = 18 sq. units

P = 22 units
A = 20 sq. units

P = 20 units
A = 18 sq. units

P = 16 units
A = 10 sq. units

P = 22 units
A = 18 sq. units

P = 20 units
A = 24 sq. units

P = 26 units
A = 20 sq. units

P = 20 units
A = 13 sq. units

P = 28 units
A = 15 sq. units

Page 61

Place +, −, x, or ÷ in each box to complete each number sentence.

4 X 5 = 20	9 + 7 = 16	9 + 8 = 17
7 − 7 = 0	4 − 1 = 3	30 ÷ 6 = 5
8 + 6 = 14	9 + 2 = 11	9 X 2 = 18
81 ÷ 9 = 9	16 ÷ 8 = 2	12 − 4 = 8
13 − 5 = 8	32 ÷ 4 = 8	54 ÷ 6 = 9
6 X 6 = 36	3 X 6 = 18	8 X 8 = 64
9 X 0 = 0	13 − 4 = 9	5 + 1 = 6
7 + 6 = 13	7 + 2 = 9	12 − 10 = 2
36 ÷ 4 = 9	20 ÷ 4 = 5	6 X 4 = 24
11 − 6 = 5	5 X 5 = 25	48 ÷ 8 = 6
8 X 7 = 56	17 − 9 = 8	2 + 8 = 10
14 − 7 = 7	72 ÷ 8 = 9	3 X 5 = 15
9 ÷ 3 = 3	3 X 4 = 12	42 ÷ 6 = 7
7 X 4 = 28	2 + 2 = 4	7 − 1 = 6
5 + 7 = 12	40 ÷ 5 = 8	8 X 3 = 24
10 − 6 = 4	7 X 7 = 49	8 + 8 = 16
16 ÷ 4 = 4	10 − 3 = 7	3 + 9 = 12
3 X 7 = 21	6 − 2 = 4	10 ÷ 5 = 2

Page 62

Use the pictograph about pets to answer the questions below.

Perky Pets   (Each picture = 2 animals)

Fish	🐟🐟🐟
Cats	🐱🐱🐱🐱🐱🐱
Gerbils	🐹
Dogs	🐕🐕🐕🐕🐕🐕🐕
Hamsters	🐹
Turtles	🐢
Birds	🐦🐦🐦
Horses	🐴🐴🐴🐴🐴

1. Write a number sentence to show the total number of dogs and cats. **14 + 12 = 26**
2. There are six of which animals? **fish + birds**
3. There are the least of which three animals? **gerbils, turtles, hamsters**
4. How many more dogs than horses are there? **4**
5. How many footless animals are shown? **6**
6. What is the total number of horses, cats, turtles, and birds shown? **32**
7. How many animal's names begin with the letter H? **2**
8. There are the most of which animals? **dogs**
9. How many more dogs than fish are there? **8**
10. What is the total number of animals shown on the pictograph? **60**

Name _____

Use the information given to fill in one vertical and one horizontal bar graph.

Vertical Bar Graph

Plot these sports balls on the graph.

6 soccer balls
14 basketballs
10 golf balls
8 softballs
16 baseballs
4 tennis balls
12 volleyballs
2 Ping-Pong balls

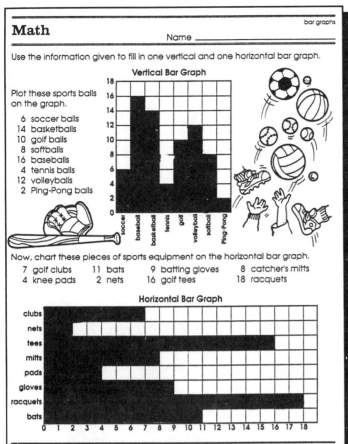

Now, chart these pieces of sports equipment on the horizontal bar graph.

7 golf clubs   11 bats   9 batting gloves   8 catcher's mitts
4 knee pads   2 nets   16 golf tees   18 racquets

Horizontal Bar Graph

Rows: clubs, nets, tees, mitts, pads, gloves, racquets, bats

Scale: 0 1 2 3 4 5 6 7 8 9 10 11 12 13 14 15 16 17 18

Name _____

Use the line graph to answer the questions.

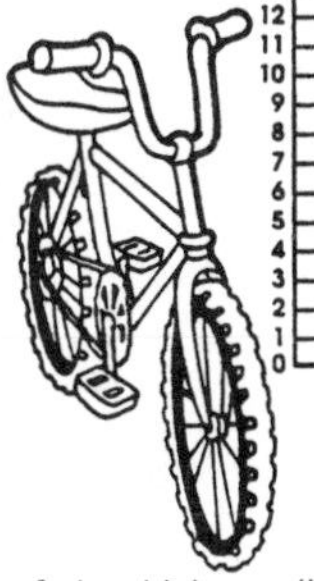

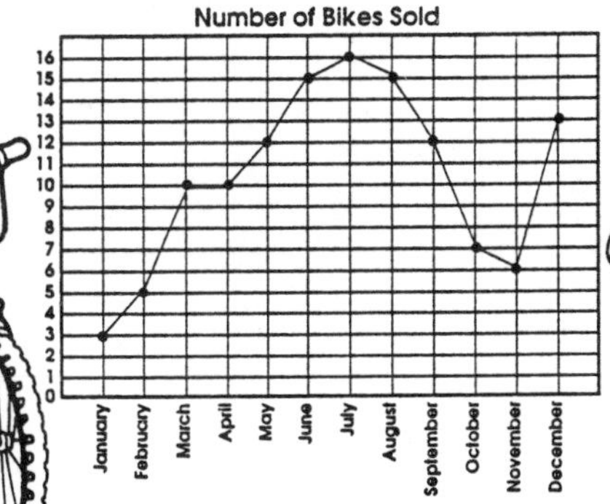

Number of Bikes Sold

(Line graph with months January through December on x-axis, values 3–16 on y-axis)

1. In which month were the most bikes sold? __July__
2. What is the total number of bikes sold in March and April? __20__
3. What is the difference between the number of bikes sold in July and those sold in October? __9__
4. In which 2 months were 15 bikes sold? __June + August__
5. In which 3 months were less than 7 sold? __Jan., Feb., Nov.__
6. In which 2 months were 12 bikes sold? __May + September__
7. What is the total of bikes sold in October, November, and December? __26__
8. In June, July, and August, how many total bikes were sold? __46__
9. In which months were more than 12 sold? __June, July, Aug., Dec.__
10. How many bikes were sold in the entire year? __124__

Name _____

Complete the multiplication grid by writing the products in the boxes.

X	4	9	0	3	8	5	1	7	2	6
2	8	18	0	6	16	10	2	14	4	12
8	32	72	0	24	64	40	8	56	16	48
1	4	9	0	3	8	5	1	7	2	6
6	24	54	0	18	48	30	6	42	12	36
7	28	63	0	21	56	35	7	49	14	42
4	16	36	0	12	32	20	4	28	8	24
0	0	0	0	0	0	0	0	0	0	0
9	36	81	0	27	72	45	9	63	18	54
5	20	45	0	15	40	25	5	35	10	30
3	12	27	0	9	24	15	3	21	6	18

Write the product for each problem.

6 ×8 = 48	5 ×4 = 20	6 ×5 = 30	4 ×7 = 28	5 ×3 = 15	4 ×4 = 16
7 ×6 = 42	8 ×3 = 24	9 ×2 = 18	6 ×4 = 24	7 ×3 = 21	8 ×4 = 32
9 ×5 = 45	3 ×4 = 12	6 ×6 = 36	7 ×5 = 35	8 ×6 = 48	4 ×5 = 20

Name _____

A magic square contains numbers that add up to the same sum, across, down, and diagonally. Fill in the numbers to make these magic squares.

8	3	4
1	5	9
6	7	2

Fill in 8, 2, 6, and 4.
The magic sum is __15__.

6	5	10
11	7	3
4	9	8

Fill in 3, 5, 9, and 7.
The magic sum is __21__.

16	2	12
6	10	14
8	18	4

Fill in 16, 12, 8, and 18.
The magic sum is __30__.

11	6	13
12	10	8
7	14	9

Fill in 9, 8, 7, and 6.
The magic sum is __30__.

8	1	6
3	5	7
4	9	2

Fill in 2, 3, 4, and 8.
The magic sum is __15__.

12	7	14
13	11	9
8	15	10

Fill in 13, 14, 10, and 11.
The magic sum is __33__.

Social Studies

Name _____

Use the compass rose to write directions for each set of arrows. Begin at the ★.

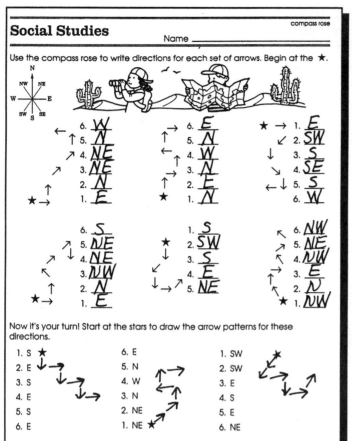

Now it's your turn! Start at the stars to draw the arrow patterns for these directions.

1. S ★
2. E
3. S
4. E
5. S
6. E

6. E
5. N
4. W
3. N
2. NE
1. NE ★

1. SW
2. SW
3. E
4. S
5. E
6. NE

Page 67

Social Studies

Name _____

Write the capital of each state by putting one letter in each section of the caterpillar. The last letter of each word will be the first letter of the next word.

1. California
2. Washington
3. Georgia
4. Maryland
5. Oregon
6. Vermont
7. Virginia
8. Colorado
9. North Carolina
10. Pennsylvania

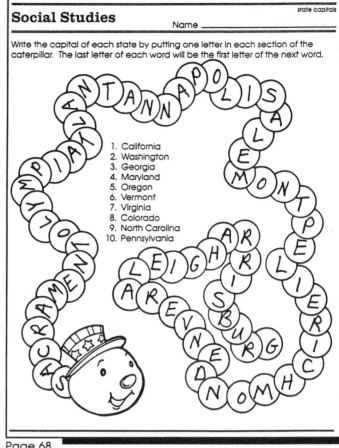

Page 68

Social Studies

Name _____

Label the continents and oceans of the four hemispheres.

Western Hemisphere

1. North America
2. South America
3. Pacific Ocean
4. Atlantic Ocean

Eastern Hemisphere

1. Europe
2. Asia
3. Africa
4. Australia
5. Antarctica
6. Indian Ocean
7. Pacific Ocean

Southern Hemisphere

1. South America
2. Africa
3. Antarctica
4. Australia
5. Atlantic Ocean
6. Indian Ocean
7. Pacific Ocean

Northern Hemisphere

1. North America
2. Asia
3. Europe
4. Africa
5. South America
6. Pacific Ocean
7. Atlantic Ocean

Page 69

Social Studies

Name _____

Follow the directions below to complete the globe.

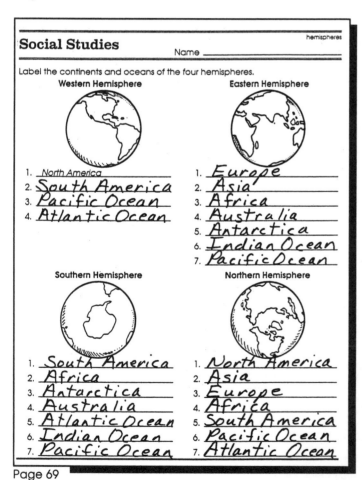

1. Draw a red line for the equator.
2. Draw a green dotted line for the prime meridian.
3. Put a purple **X** for the North Pole.
4. Put a brown **X** for the South Pole.
5. Draw four yellow lines of longitude, connecting at the North and South Poles.
6. Draw eight orange lines of latitude spaced evenly apart.
7. Name the four hemispheres. Northern   Southern   Eastern   Western
8. In which two hemispheres do you live? Northern Western

Page 70

Page 71

Create a map on the grid by following the directions below.

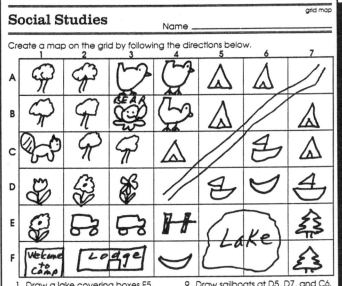

1. Draw a lake covering boxes E5, E6, F5, and F6.
2. Put evergreen trees in E7 and F7.
3. Draw a pier at E4.
4. Put canoes at D6 and F4.
5. Add tour buses at E2 and E3.
6. Draw a lodge covering F2 and F3.
7. Draw a "Welcome to Camp" sign at F1.
8. Draw a flower garden covering D1, D2, D3, and E1.
9. Draw sailboats at D5, D7, and C6.
10. Draw a diagonal path cutting through D4, C5, B6, and A7.
11. Put tents at C4, A5, A6, B5, B7, and C7.
12. Draw a bear at B3.
13. Draw a raccoon in C1.
14. Draw a forest covering A1, A2, B1, B2, C2, and C3.
15. Draw birds in A3, A4, and B4.

Page 72

The letters and numbers on the grid are called coordinates. Use the coordinates to find who's who at the zoo.

1. The elephants are found in *E6*, *E7*, *D7*.
2. What would you do at A3 and A4? *Get food*
3. Where are the monkeys? *D1*, *E1*, *E2*.
4. What would you see at A5 and B5? *Birds*
5. Where is the gorilla? *D2*
6. To what animal family do those in A6, A7, B6, and B7 belong? *cats*
7. Where would you find kangaroos? *C7*
8. Where could you picnic? *B3*, *B4*, *C3*, *C4*

9. What would you see at C2? *RHINO*
10. Where would you see snakes? *A1, A2, B2*
11. Lizards are found at *B1*
12. What would you see at C1? *HIPPO*
13. Where would you go to see water animals? *D3, D4, E4*
14. What is at E3? *ORANGUTAN*
15. Bears could be found at *C5, D5, E5, D6*
16. Where are the giraffes? *C6*

Page 73

Use the latitude and longitude coordinates to answer each question.

1. What line of longitude passes through the middle of the waterslide? *110°E*
2. The roller coaster goes between what lines of latitude? *50°N–20°N*
3. The carousel crosses which longitude line? *120°E*
4. To go from the pop stand to the cotton candy, which longitude lines do you cross? *110°E, 120°E, 130°E*
5. From the Pirate's Ship to the Dodge 'Em Cars, you pass which lines of latitude? *40°N, 30°N*
6. The sand dunes lie between which lines of longitude? *100°E – 80°E*
7. The kiddie rides are between *40°N* and *50°N* latitude and *120°E* and *110°E* longitude.
8. From the beach to the sand dunes, you cross what latitude lines? *40°N*
9. If you cross 40°N from the hotdog stand, where are you? *Pirate Ship*
10. The nachos are between *20°N* and *30°N* latitude, and *120°E* and *110°E* longitude.
11. Which line of longitude passes through the center of the Log Ride? *110°E*
12. Which longitude line do you pass to go from the entrance gate to the ticket booth? *140°E*

Page 75

Use with page 74.

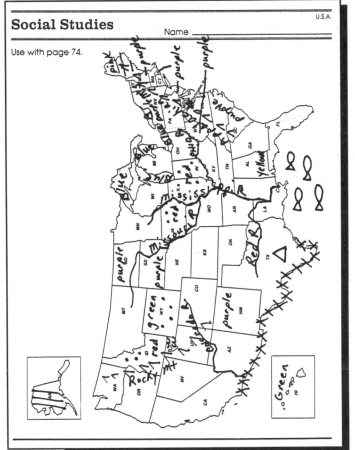

Social Studies

Name _____

Follow the directions to create a banner of our national symbols.

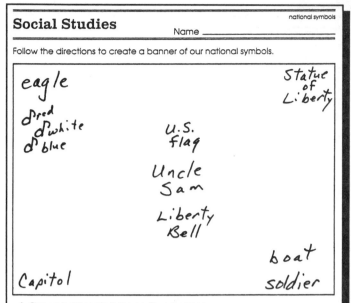

1. Draw a bald eagle in the northwest corner.
2. Draw a soldier to represent Yankee Doodle in the southeast corner.
3. Draw Uncle Sam in the middle.
4. Draw the Statue of Liberty in the northeast corner.
5. Draw the Capitol building in the southwest corner.
6. Draw the Liberty Bell below Uncle Sam.
7. Draw our nation's flag above Uncle Sam.
8. Below the eagle, draw three musical notes—one red, one white, and one blue— to represent the Star Spangled Banner.
9. Above Yankee Doodle, draw a boat to represent the Boston Tea Party.

Social Studies

Name _____

Write the number of each Washington, D.C. attraction in the box by its picture. Choose two attractions to write a report on.

1. Lincoln Memorial
2. Vietnam Veterans Memorial
3. Washington Monument
4. Supreme Court Building
5. United States Capitol
6. White House
7. Arlington National Cemetery
8. Jefferson Memorial
9. Museum of Natural History
10. The Marine Corps War Memorial
11. Ford's Theater
12. Air and Space Museum

Social Studies

Name _____

Write the name of each state next to its two-letter abbreviation.

1. CT Connecticut
2. DE Delaware
3. AK Alaska
4. ME Maine
5. MD Maryland
6. MA Massachusetts
7. NH New Hampshire
8. NJ New Jersey
9. NY New York
10. PA Pennsylvania
11. RI Rhode Island
12. VT Vermont
13. WV West Virginia
14. AL Alabama
15. AR Arkansas
16. FL Florida
17. GA Georgia
18. KY Kentucky
19. HI Hawaii
20. LA Louisiana
21. MS Mississippi
22. NC North Carolina
23. SC South Carolina
24. TN Tennessee
25. VA Virginia
26. IL Illinois
27. IN Indiana
28. IA Iowa
29. MI Michigan
30. MN Minnesota
31. MO Missouri
32. OH Ohio
33. WI Wisconsin
34. KS Kansas
35. NE Nebraska
36. ND North Dakota
37. OK Oklahoma
38. SD South Dakota
39. TX Texas
40. AZ Arizona
41. CA California
42. CO Colorado
43. ID Idaho
44. MT Montana
45. NV Nevada
46. NM New Mexico
47. OR Oregon
48. UT Utah
49. WA Washington
50. WY Wyoming

Social Studies

Name _____

Unscramble the names of these physical features found in our country. Then use the numbers to label the map below.

1. nailds   island
2. utimoann mountain
3. spalnnieu peninsula
4. aplin   plain
5. canoe   ocean
6. drober   border
7. fulg   gulf
8. virer   river
9. elka   lake
10. tacos   coast

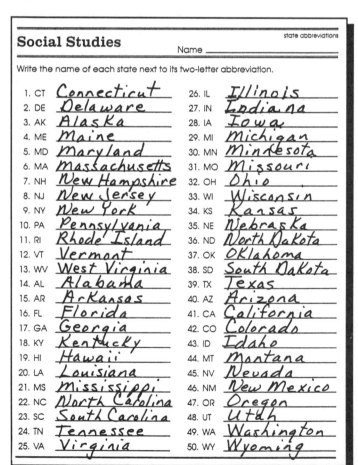

© Instructional Fair, Inc.   122   IF8785 Third Grade in Review

Social Studies

Name _____

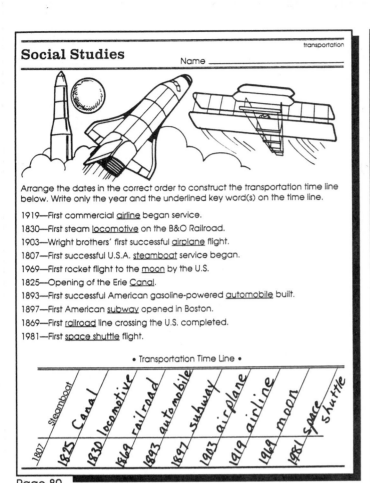

Arrange the dates in the correct order to construct the transportation time line below. Write only the year and the underlined key word(s) on the time line.

1919—First commercial <u>airline</u> began service.
1830—First steam <u>locomotive</u> on the B&O Railroad.
1903—Wright brothers' first successful <u>airplane</u> flight.
1807—First successful U.S.A. <u>steamboat</u> service began.
1969—First rocket flight to the <u>moon</u> by the U.S.
1825—Opening of the Erie <u>Canal</u>.
1893—First successful American gasoline-powered <u>automobile</u> built.
1897—First American <u>subway</u> opened in Boston.
1869—First <u>railroad</u> line crossing the U.S. completed.
1981—First <u>space shuttle</u> flight.

• Transportation Time Line •

1807	1825	1830	1869	1893	1897	1903	1919	1969	1981
steamboat	Canal	locomotive	railroad	automobile	subway	airplane	airline	moon	space shuttle

Page 80

Social Studies

Name _____

Number the events telling of the history of U.S. communication in order. Then illustrate each one in the correct box.

8 In 1953, color telecasts began.
1 The first public subscription library in the U.S. was founded in 1731.
4 Samuel Morse first publicly demonstrated the telegraph in 1837.
7 The U.S. began regular TV broadcasts in 1939.
2 In 1741, the first magazine was published in the U.S.
5 Alexander Graham Bell patented the first successful telephone in 1876.
3 In 1833, the first successful penny newspaper was published in New York.
6 The first regular radio broadcasts began in 1920.

3	6	1	7
4	8	2	5

Page 81

Social Studies

Name _____

Read each clue. Circle the name of the corresponding holiday in the wordsearch. Use the color given.

1. Honors our first president   (purple)
2. Celebrates the discovery of our country   (green)
3. Our country's birthday—July 4, 1776   (blue)
4. Honors the banner of the U.S.   (red)
5. A holiday to give thanks   (orange)
6. Honors those who died in past wars   (black)
7. Remembers the president who put an end to slavery   (yellow)
8. Remembers the man who fought peacefully for civil rights   (pink)
9. Honors our country's workers   (brown)

G	A	S	H	T	G	O	N	Q	R	S	D	E	T	R	A	L	G	B	E	D
R	G	K	L	D	I	N	G	S	T	O	N	S	B	I	R	D	A	T	H	G
E	Y	E	L	L	O	W	L	N	S	B	I	R	T	H	D	A	L	A	B	E	R
E	F	T	O	N	S	R	L	E	G	R	H	A	Y	I	D	A	N	V	I	N
N	K	R	N	K	L	D	E	U	T	H	E	R	K	I	N	G	J	R	D	A
D	V	T	H	A	D	G	R	Y	D	A	Y	F	L	O	G	R	T	Y	A
A	S	B	A	B	L	U	E	P	E	N	D	E	N	C	D	A	D	A
D	R	L	T	U	T	H	E	R	K	I	G	D	A	M	Y	L	A	O	N
A	O	D	H	L	I	N	C	O	L	N	S	D	T	Y	L	U	T	H
V	D	P	U	R	P	L	E	T	O	N	S	B	I	T	H	D	A
G	N	S	W	C	O	L	U	M	B	D	Y	T	U	V	N	G	R	T	S
I	E	K	C	A	R	L	D	W	A	S	H	I	W	A	T	O	N	B	I
U	I	O	R	A	N	G	E	S	G	I	V	I	N	R	A	A	L	I	G	E
I	A	S	M	E	M	O	R	L	I	N	D	E	W	C	O	L	U	M
N	T	U	L	X	T	O	B	R	E	J	D	E	A	N	L	U	T	H	E
T	H	A	K	S	G	A	V	I	N	D	Y	B	I	R	T	H	D	A	W

Page 82

Science

Name _____

Plants and animals are living things called organisms. They have five features in common. Unscramble the sentences to identify these features.

1. to must they able grow be
   They must be able to grow.

2. cells of made are they more or one
   They are made of one or more cells

3. need they food
   They need food.

4. their environment to they respond
   They respond to their environment.

5. can reproduce they
   They can reproduce.

Color only the pictures of the things with the five features.

Page 83

Page 84

Science
Name _____

All organisms pass through life cycles with varying numbers of stages. The monarch butterfly has four stages in its life cycle. Unscramble each word to identify the stages.

Stage 1: g e g _egg_

Laid on plants, some are smaller than a pinhead

Stage 2: l i a r c e t a p r l _caterpillar_

Most are green or brown, last at least two weeks, shed skin 4-5 times

Stage 3: a p p u _pupa_

Shell that forms around the caterpillar and hardens

Stage 4: t d l u a f u t r e l b y t _adult butterfly_

Emerges from pupa, lives from a week or two to 18 months

Now draw **your** life cycle—past, present, and future.

Baby	Toddler	Child	Teenager	Adult

Page 85

Science
Name _____

Place the animals listed below in the correct family by writing their names on the lines.

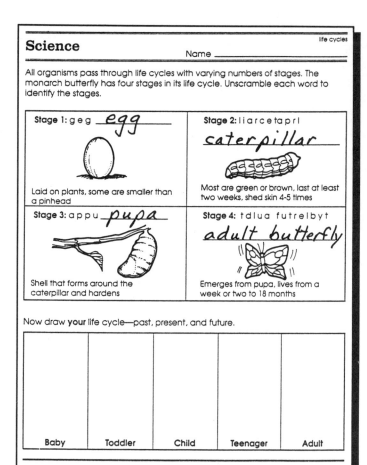

Fish
perch
trout
salmon
shark

Amphibians
frog
salamander
newt

Insects
ladybug
grasshopper
dragonfly
beetle

Reptiles
alligator
cobra
rattlesnake
crocodile
lizard

Birds
parrot
robin
flamingo
penguin
peacock

Mammals
horse
whale
dog
raccoon

alligator	trout	rattlesnake	flamingo	raccoon
perch	whale	ladybug	salmon	newt
parrot	robin	crocodile	dragonfly	shark
horse	dog	salamander	lizard	penguin
cobra	frog	grasshopper	peacock	beetle

Page 86

Science
Name _____

A habitat is an animal's home. Choose an animal from the Word Bank that might live in each habitat.

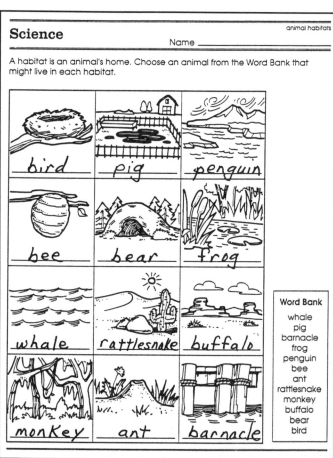

bird   pig   penguin

bee   bear   frog

whale   rattlesnake   buffalo

monkey   ant   barnacle

Word Bank
whale
pig
barnacle
frog
penguin
bee
ant
rattlesnake
monkey
buffalo
bear
bird

Page 87

Science
Name _____

Endangered animals are those which may not survive. Extinct animals are no longer living. Use the code to identify these endangered or extinct animals.

A	B	C	D	E	F	G	H	I	J	K	L	M
3	17	8	11	1	23	14	19	4	26	21	13	7

N	O	P	Q	R	S	T	U	V	W	X	Y	Z
9	2	15	20	10	6	12	5	18	24	22	16	25

Endangered Animals
1. 17-3-13-11   1-3-14-13-1   _Bald Eagle_
2. 10-1-11   24-2-13-23   _Red Wolf_
3. 23-13-2-10-4-11-3   15-3-9-12-19-1-10   _Florida Panther_
4. 24-2-2-11   17-4-6-2-9   _Wood Bison_
5. 7-4-6-6-4-2-9,   17-13-5-1   17-5-12-12-1-10-23-13-16   _Mission Blue Butterfly_
6. 8-3-13-4-23-2-10-9-4-3   8-2-9-11-2-10   _California Condor_
7. 6-12-1-13-13-1-10-6   6-1-3   13-4-2-9   _Stellers Sea Lion_
8. 2-8-1-13-2-12   _Ocelot_
9. 14-10-4-25-25-13-16   17-1-3-10   _Grizzly Bear_
10. 24-19-2-2-15-4-9-14   8-10-3-9-1   _Whooping Crane_

Extinct Animals
1. 11-4-9-2-6-3-5-10   _Dinosaur_
2. 7-2-3   _Moa_
3. 15-3-6-6-1-9-14-1-10   15-4-14-1-2-9   _Passenger Pigeon_
4. 6-12-1-13-13-1-10-6   6-1-3   8-2-24   _Stellers Sea Cow_
5. 24-2-2-13-16   7-3-7-7-2-12-19   _Woolly Mammoth_
6. 13-3-17-10-3-11-2-10   11-5-8-21   _Labrador Duck_
7. 11-2-11-2   17-4-10-11   _Dodo Bird_
8. 14-10-1-3-12   3-5-21   _Great Auk_

Page 88

Science

Name _____

Many plants grow from seeds. Label the seed parts—developing plant, stored food, and seed coat.

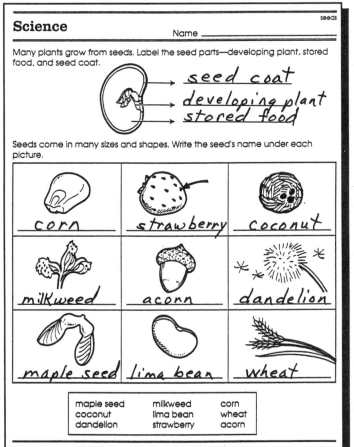

seed coat
developing plant
stored food

Seeds come in many sizes and shapes. Write the seed's name under each picture.

corn	_strawberry_	_coconut_
milkweed	_acorn_	_dandelion_
maple seed	_lima bean_	_wheat_

maple seed	milkweed	corn
coconut	lima bean	wheat
dandelion	strawberry	acorn

Page 88

Page 89

Science

Name _____

Plants give us many things we need. Follow the numbers to write some things plants give us.

1. 10 6 5 1 2 7 8 4 3 9
    s a t v e b l e g e

2. 6 5 4 2 1 3
    r e b u l m

3. 4 2 5 6 1 3
    i r t s f u

4. 4 2 1 5 3 6
    t o c o t n

5. 2 1 4 3 5
    a p e p r

6. 4 2 6 5 3 1
    b u r e b r

7. 4 5 2 1 6 3
    g e x o n y

8. 3 2 4 5 1   5 4 3 1 2
    p a l e m   p u r s y

9. 2 5 1 3 4
    i n l n e

10. 4 3 2 5 1 6
    c i p e s s

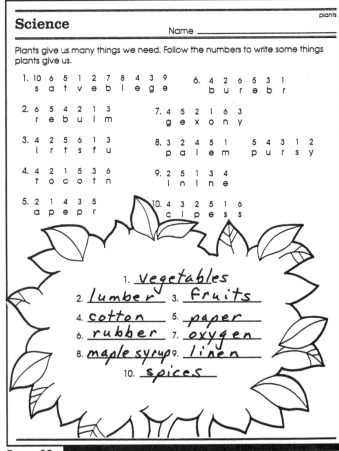

1. _vegetables_
2. _lumber_ 3. _fruits_
4. _cotton_ 5. _paper_
6. _rubber_ 7. _oxygen_
8. _maple syrup_ 9. _linen_
10. _spices_

Page 89

Page 90

Science

Name _____

There are many kinds of energy. Use the key to mark the kind of energy each object produces.

H= heat	S = sound	M = motion
L = light	E = electricity	

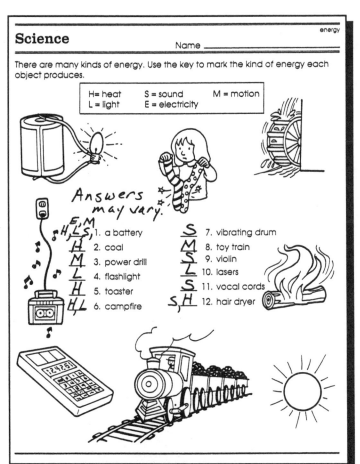

Answers may vary.

E, M
H, L, S   1. a battery
H   2. coal
M   3. power drill
L   4. flashlight
H   5. toaster
H, L   6. campfire

S   7. vibrating drum
M   8. toy train
S   9. violin
L   10. lasers
S   11. vocal cords
S, H   12. hair dryer

Page 90

Page 91

Science

Name _____

Use the weather words from the Weather Bank to work the puzzle.

Weather Bank			
predict	thermometer	dew	windy
cloud	smog	blizzard	thunder
icicle	hurricane	tornado	snow
precipitation	frost	rain	sleet

Across:
2. to foretell upcoming weather
3. used to measure temperature
5. frozen water vapor
6. a collection of water droplets high in the air
8. a heavy, windy, blinding snowstorm
9. needlelike frozen water
10. a windy funnel-shaped storm
11. water vapor condensing on a cool object
12. breezy
13. liquid precipitation
14. solid, flaky precipitation

Down:
1. smoke and fog
2. water that falls to earth
4. a storm that forms over an ocean
7. partially frozen rain
10. the sound that follows lightning

Crossword answers: SMOG, PREDICT, THERMOMETER, HURRICANE, FROST, CLOUD, BLIZZARD, ICICLE, SLEET, TORNADO, DEW, WINDY, RAIN, SNOW, PRECIPITATION

Page 91

Science

Name _____

Write the name of the correct planet by each clue.

Pluto	Venus	Saturn
Neptune	Uranus	Mercury
Earth	Jupiter	Mars

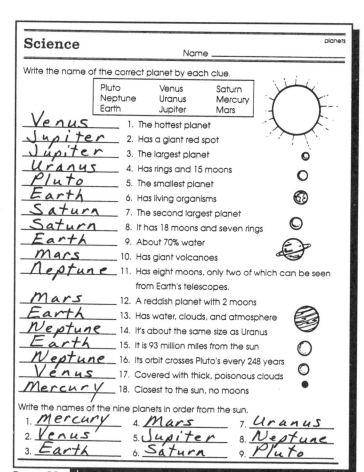

Venus — 1. The hottest planet
Jupiter — 2. Has a giant red spot
Jupiter — 3. The largest planet
Uranus — 4. Has rings and 15 moons
Pluto — 5. The smallest planet
Earth — 6. Has living organisms
Saturn — 7. The second largest planet
Saturn — 8. It has 18 moons and seven rings
Earth — 9. About 70% water
Mars — 10. Has giant volcanoes
Neptune — 11. Has eight moons, only two of which can be seen from Earth's telescopes.
Mars — 12. A reddish planet with 2 moons
Earth — 13. Has water, clouds, and atmosphere
Neptune — 14. It's about the same size as Uranus
Earth — 15. It is 93 million miles from the sun
Neptune — 16. Its orbit crosses Pluto's every 248 years
Venus — 17. Covered with thick, poisonous clouds
Mercury — 18. Closest to the sun, no moons

Write the names of the nine planets in order from the sun.

1. *Mercury*   4. *Mars*   7. *Uranus*
2. *Venus*   5. *Jupiter*   8. *Neptune*
3. *Earth*   6. *Saturn*   9. *Pluto*

Page 92

Science

Name _____

Create a car of the future by combining these simple machines. Use at least one of each kind. Name your new model.

Car of the Future

Cars will vary.

Model Name _____

Page 93

Science

Name _____

Read each clue and then write the matching scientist on the line.

1. I study the stars and other celestial bodies. *astronomer*	6. I study the effects of electricity. *electrical engineer*
2. I work with chemical combinations. *chemist*	7. I help preserve animals' habitats. *conservationist*
3. I am a space traveler. *astronaut*	8. I study all forms of animal life. *zoologist*
4. I study the earth's physical features. *geologist*	9. I study fossil remains. *paleontologist*
5. I study and predict the weather. *meteorologist*	10. I study plant life. *botanist*

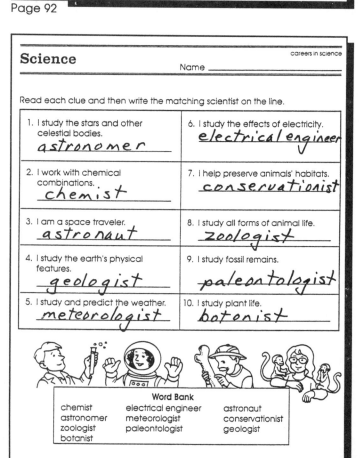

Word Bank

chemist	electrical engineer	astronaut
astronomer	meteorologist	conservationist
zoologist	paleontologist	geologist
botanist		

Page 94

Health

Name _____

Draw the number of servings needed daily from each food group.

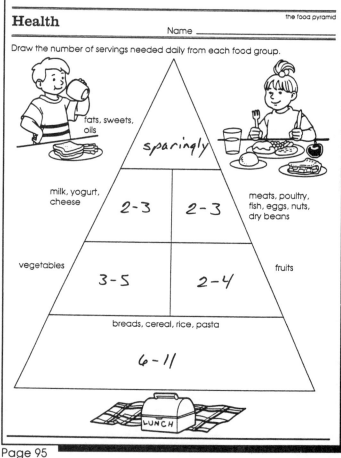

fats, sweets, oils — *sparingly*

milk, yogurt, cheese — *2-3*

meats, poultry, fish, eggs, nuts, dry beans — *2-3*

vegetables — *3-5*

fruits — *2-4*

breads, cereal, rice, pasta — *6-11*

Page 95

Health

Name _____

Decorate this checkered tablecloth. Decide the food group to which each of these foods belongs. Color according to the pyramid key to the right.

Pyramid key:
- other (purple)
- dairy (yellow) / meats (red)
- vegetables (blue) / fruits (green)
- grains (brown)

Blue potato	Red turkey	Purple cake	Blue onion	Yellow milk	Blue pickle
Green peach	Red eggs	Green watermelon	Red bologna	Green apple	Blue carrot
Red hot dog	Blue beet	Yellow yogurt	Green grapes	Red hamburger	Brown bun
Brown bread	Red ham	Blue cucumber	Yellow cheddar cheese	Purple brownie	Red peanuts
Red chicken	Purple candy bar	Brown bagel	Blue lettuce	Red steak	Green banana
Green cherry	Red walnuts	Red bacon	Green pineapple	Green orange	Yellow sour cream
Yellow cream cheese	Blue lima beans	Brown crackers	Yellow ice cream	Blue corn	Brown rice
Brown macaroni	Red pork chop	Blue cabbage	Brown biscuits	Green lemon	Yellow butter
Blue spinach	Purple donut	Green nectarine	Red ham	Green plum	Green strawberry
Blue green beans	Red pecans	Yellow cream	Brown spaghetti	Purple Popsicle™	Red veal

Page 96

Health

Name _____

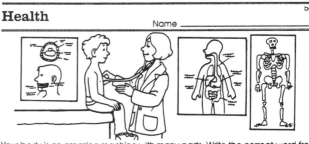

Your body is an amazing machine with many parts. Write the correct word from the Word Bank in each blank.

Word Bank
enamel	fingerprint	bones
hairs	nerve fibers	colors
water	blood vessels	beats
skin	muscles	

1. Half of the 200 __bones__ in your body are in your hands and feet.
2. __Muscles__ make up half of the weight of your body.
3. __Skin__ is the largest organ in the human body.
4. Tooth __enamel__ is the hardest substance in your body.
5. Messages travel along your __nerve fibers__ at 3 to 300 feet per second.
6. Your eyes can distinguish more than 200 __colors__ .
7. Your heart __beats__ about 36 million times a year.
8. An average person has 100,000 __hairs__ on his head.
9. The body is made of about 65% __water__ .
10. Your __blood vessels__ could branch out 60,000 miles.
11. No two people have the same pattern of loops, whorls, or arches in their __fingerprint__

Page 97

Health

Name _____

Show what you know about teeth. Label each box using words from the Word Bank.

Word Bank
cavity	pulp	toothpaste
floss	crown	calcium
plaque	root	primary teeth
gums	enamel	permanent teeth

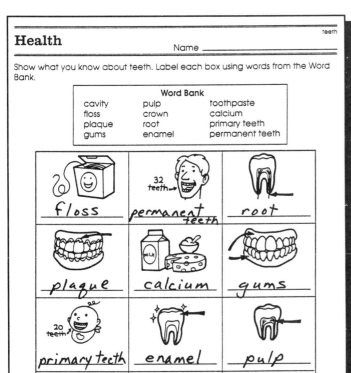

floss | permanent teeth | root
plaque | calcium | gums
primary teeth | enamel | pulp
crown | toothpaste | cavity

Page 98

Health

Name _____

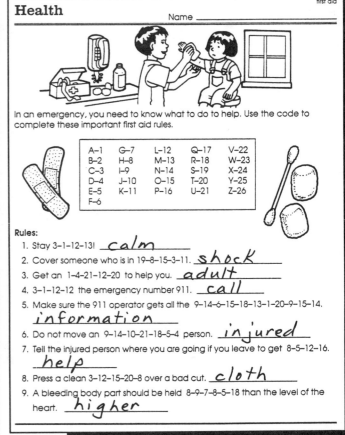

In an emergency, you need to know what to do to help. Use the code to complete these important first aid rules.

A–1	G–7	L–12	Q–17	V–22
B–2	H–8	M–13	R–18	W–23
C–3	I–9	N–14	S–19	X–24
D–4	J–10	O–15	T–20	Y–25
E–5	K–11	P–16	U–21	Z–26
F–6				

Rules:
1. Stay 3–1–12–13! __calm__
2. Cover someone who is in 19–8–15–3–11. __shock__
3. Get an 1–4–21–12–20 to help you. __adult__
4. 3–1–12–12 the emergency number 911. __call__
5. Make sure the 911 operator gets all the 9–14–6–15–18–13–1–20–9–15–14. __information__
6. Do not move an 9–14–10–21–18–5–4 person. __injured__
7. Tell the injured person where you are going if you leave to get 8–5–12–16. __help__
8. Press a clean 3–12–15–20–8 over a bad cut. __cloth__
9. A bleeding body part should be held 8–9–7–8–5–18 than the level of the heart. __higher__

Page 99

Name _____

A well-groomed person has a neat and clean appearance. Try keeping this grooming chart for one week. Place a ☺ for each well-done task, a 😐 for a task done but not well, and a 😞 for one not done or done poorly. After one week, evaluate your chart and work on your weaker areas.

Task	Sunday	Monday	Tuesday	Wednes-day	Thursday	Friday	Saturday
1. shower or bathe		*Answers*					
2. wear clean clothes		*will*					
3. brush teeth 3 times a day		*vary.*					
4. sleep at least 8 hours							
5. wash hair							
6. comb or brush hair							
7. exercise for 1 hour							
8. floss once							

Name _____

Smart kids follow safety rules to remain healthy and safe. Draw the correct code symbol next to each rule.

car safety — water safety — walking safety — bike safety — poison safety

- *car* 1. Get in and out on the curb side of a parked car.
- *poison* 2. Keep labels on all containers.
- *bike* 3. Wear white when riding in twilight.
- *walking* 4. Always walk on sidewalks, not in the street.
- *bike* 5. Ride in the same direction as the moving cars.
- *bike* 6. Be sure your bike is in good working order.
- *poison* 7. Tighten caps on containers after using.
- *water* 8. Do not run on swimming pool decks.
- *car bike* 9. Stay back at railroad crossings.
- *bike walking* 10. Look both ways before crossing a road.
- *water* 11. Always wear a life preserver while boating.
- *bike* 12. Be sure your bike has lights and reflectors.
- *poison* 13. Keep the poison control number near your phone.
- *water* 14. Always swim with a buddy.
- *walking* 15. While walking, follow traffic lights and signs.
- *car* 16. Always keep car doors locked.
- *water* 17. Swim only in approved marked areas with an adult present.
- *bike walking* 18. Cross streets only at corners.

Name _____

Read each riddle to identify the health career worker. Write the career in each box.

I check eyes and prescribe glasses when needed. *optometrist*	I warn of the dangers of drugs and alcohol. *drug counselor*	I fit teeth for braces and other appliances. *orthodontist*
I check to see that all body systems are working properly. *doctor*	I supervise exercise programs. *fitness coach*	I plan well-balanced meals for good nutrition. *dietician*
I check feet for problems. *podiatrist*	I help solve emotional problems. *psychologist*	I clean teeth and make needed repairs. *dentist*
I keep athletes' bodies in good physical condition. *sports medicine*	I repair bones when they are broken. *orthopedist*	I fill prescriptions written by doctors for medicine. *pharmacist*

Word Bank		
orthodontist	doctor	podiatrist
psychologist	optometrist	drug counselor
dietician	pharmacist	sports medicine
dentist	orthopedist	fitness coach

About the Book

This is a great activity book which can be used in the spring for review, or in the summer or fall to brush up on skills from the previous year. The author has used a variety of activities which every child will enjoy while reviewing Language Arts, Math, Health and Science and Social Studies.

Credits

Author: Jan Kennedy
Artist: Catherine Yuh
Project Director/Editor: Sue Sutton
Editors: Alyson Kieda, Louise Benzer
*Cover Photo: Frank Pieroni
Production: Pat Geasler

* Cover photo taken of the Rounds School in Rockford, MI. Permission to use given by the Rockford Rotary Club.